W9-BKG-268

Cross-Stitch
in Blue
& White

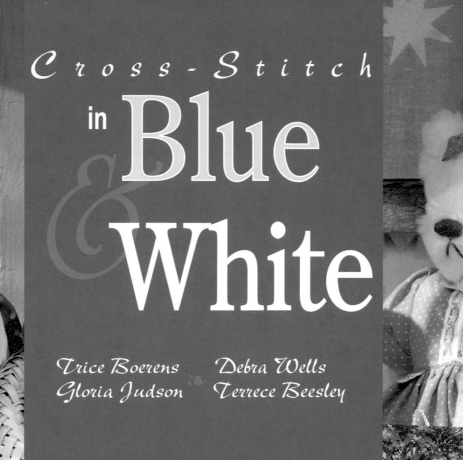

Cross-Stitch
in Blue
& White

Trice Boerens   *Debra Wells*
Gloria Judson   *Terrece Beesley*

Sterling Publishing Co., Inc. New York
A Sterling/Chapelle Book

For Chapelle Limited

Owner: Jo Packham

Designers: Terrece Beesley, Trice Boerens,
Gloria Judson, and Debra Wells

Staff: Malissa Boatwright, Rebecca Christensen,
Kellie Valentine-Cracas, Holly Fuller,
Amber Hansen, Cherie Hanson, Holly Hollingsworth,
Susan Jorgensen, Susan Laws, Amanda McPeck,
Barbara Milburn, Jamie Pierce, Leslie Ridenour, Cindy Rooks,
Cindy Stoeckl, Nancy Whitley and Lorrie Young

Photographer: Kevin Dilley for Hazen Photography
Styling: Cherie Herrick

Special thanks to Terry Johnson for allowing us to use her beautiful
miniature furniture. Her trust is greatly appreciated.

For information on where you can purchase specialty items in this book, please write to:

Customer Service Department
Chapelle Limited
204 25th Street, Suite 300
Ogden, UT 84401

Library of Congress Cataloging-in-Publication Data

Cross-stitch in blue & white / Trice Boerens ... [et al.].
p.   cm.
"A Sterling-Chapelle book."
Includes index.
ISBN 0-8069-0326-0
1. Cross-stitch–Patterns.   2. Blue in art.   3. White in art.
I. Boerens, Trice.
TT778.3C76C767   1995
746.44'3041–dc20

1 3 5 7 9 10 8 6 4 2

A Sterling/Chapelle Book

Published by Sterling Publishing Company, Inc.
387 Park Avenue South, New York, N.Y. 10016
© 1995 by Chapelle Ltd.
Distributed in Canada by Sterling Publishing
c⁄o Canadian Manda Group, One Atlantic Avenue, Suite 105
Toronto, Ontario, Canada M6K 3E7
Distributed in Great Britain and Europe by Cassell PLC
Wellington House, 125 Strand, London WC2R 0BB, England
Distributed in Australia by Capricorn Link (Australia) Pty Ltd.
P.O. Box 6651, Baulkham Hills, Business Centre, NSW 2153, Australia
Printed and bound in Hong Kong
All Rights Reserved

Sterling ISBN 0-8069-0326-0

Introduction

Cross-Stitch in Blue & White is a peek into the sketchbooks of four talented artists. Each of these women shares her own creativity, individual style and emotions through an array of blue-and-white designs.

Stitchers are invited to peer into each artist's well of inspiration and to be carried away in the flow of the creative juices that pour out into a smooth combination of four styles, reflected in 37 different pieces—all designed and stitched in various shades of blue and white.

It would seem that creating with only two colors would prove limiting to the designer. However, the pieces presented communicate a wide range of feelings to which the color blue is often referred. Images spring into our mind when we hear phrases such as "true-blue," "blue eyes," "baby-blue," "out of the blue," "skies of blue," "deep-blue," "blue-blooded," "blue jeans," "singing the blues," "blue ribbon"—even "turning blue." Each of these conjures up a completely different mood and message. Expression is the goal of each artist.

Trice Boerens begins with fanciful and delicate designs. Next, the stitcher moves to the realistic, comforting compositions of Debra Wells and is then introduced to a decidedly different theme which is cast in the work of Gloria Judson, the third artist. Her style and use of colors are bold and stylized with a feel for the country. Terrece Beesley winds up the tour with rich designs that use an intricate variety of colors—all of them shades of blue.

From classic, to contemporary, to country, *Cross-Stitch in Blue & White* is certain to have the piece that will best express your own mood—whether as exuberant as "blue skies" or as somber as "the blues."

Contents

Contents

Trice Boerens

I was raised in Ogden, Utah, where I make my home with my husband and four children. Creative inspiration comes to me from many sources. One of these is the time that I spend in the company of friends and family (I also have four sisters).

My home serves as my art studio as well as the place where I care for my growing family. In an ideal world, I would rather spend time reading and painting instead of doing laundry.

A combination of the techniques I've studied personalizes my surroundings. Mixing textures and colors provides my art with contrast and—at the same time—harmony. Within my home, I am at ease blending quilted wall hangings, framed art- and needlework, and intriguing potteries with classic rugs, leathers and warm woods, producing a style that is all my own. It's exciting to experiment with new mediums. Muted colors are my preference, whether they are displayed in art-work, home decorating or in the clothing I wear.

I graduated from Brigham Young University with a degree in graphic arts. I have been designing for The Vanessa-Ann Collection, which is a division of Chapelle Limited, for more than 13 years.

I enjoy working with numerous artistic mediums, including watercolor, colored pencil, ink, wood, and fabric. Currently, I am very interested in combining printmaking techniques—that is, block printing and silk screening—with fabric.

9

Hydrangea Planter

Stitched on white Belfast linen 32 over 2 threads, the finished design size is 3¼" x 2" for one motif. The fabric was cut 14" x 5".

Fabric	Design Size
Aida 11	4¾" x 2⅞"
Aida 14	3¾" x 2¼"
Aida 18	3" x 1¾"
Hardanger	2⅜" x 1⅜"

Anchor **DMC (used for sample)**

Step 1: Cross-stitch (2 strands)

Anchor	Symbol	DMC	Color
158	•	775	Baby Blue-vy. lt.
160	○	813	Blue-lt.
167	△	3766	Peacock Blue-lt.
978	–	322	Navy Blue-vy. lt.
147	□	312	Navy Blue-lt.
127	●	939	Navy Blue-vy. dk.
398	×	415	Pearl Gray

Step 2: Backstitch (1 strand)

Anchor	DMC	Color
127	939	Navy Blue-vy. dk.

Hydrangea Planter (Top) **Stitch count: 53 x 31 (one motif)**

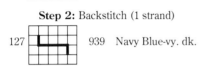

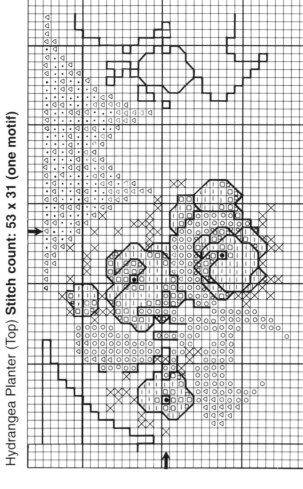

Hydrangea and Azalea Planters

Materials

Purchased corner planter painted as desired
Finished design trimmed 1" larger than front panel of planter
Matching cording to fit around design
Lightweight cardboard
Spray adhesive
Hot glue gun and glue sticks

Directions

1. Trim lightweight cardboard to fit front panel of planter. Spray front of cardboard with adhesive and mount finished design, folding and gluing edges to back.

2. Hot-glue cross-stitch panel to front of planter. Glue cording around edges.

Azalea Planter

Stitched on antique white Belfast linen 32 over 2 threads, the finished design size for one motif is 2½" x 1¾". The fabric was cut 14" x 5".

Fabric	Design Size
Aida 11	3¾" x 2½"
Aida 14	2⅞" x 2"
Aida 18	2¼" x 1½"
Hardanger	1⅞" x 1¼"

Azalea Planter **Stitch count: 41 x 28 (one motif)**

Anchor **DMC (used for sample)**

Step 1: Cross-stitch (2 strands)

Anchor	Symbol	DMC	Color
158	•	3756	Baby Blue-ultra vy. lt.
159	○	827	Blue-vy. lt.
160	□	813	Blue-lt.
167	△	3766	Peacock Blue-lt.
922	∴	930	Antique Blue-dk.
117	–	341	Blue Violet-lt.
118	×	340	Blue Violet-med.

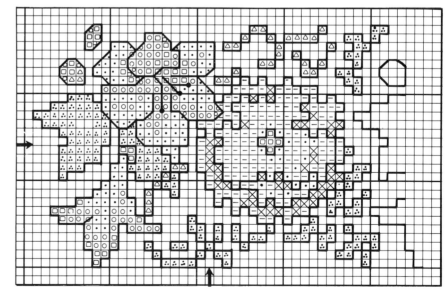

Step 2: Backstitch (1 strand)

Anchor	DMC	Color
922	930	Antique Blue-dk.

Step 3: French Knot (1 strand)

Anchor	DMC	Color
922	930	Antique Blue-dk.

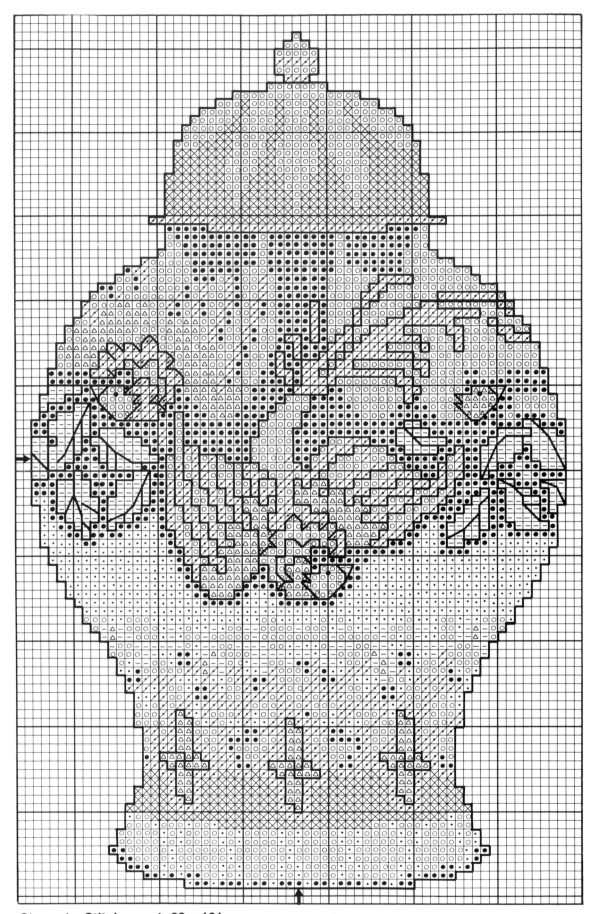

Ginger Jar **Stitch count: 63 x 101**

Ginger Jar

Stitched on white Murano 30 over 2 threads, the finished design size is 4¼" x 6¾". The fabric was cut 11" x 13". See photo on page 12.

Fabric	Design Size
Aida 11	5¾" x 9⅛"
Aida 14	4½" x 7¼"
Aida 18	3½" x 5⅝"
Hardanger	2⅞" x 4⅝"

Anchor **DMC (used for sample)**

Step 1: Cross-stitch (2 strands)

Anchor	Symbol	DMC	Color
1	–		White
343	/	3752	Antique Blue-ultra vy. lt.
130	△	809	Delft
160	·	813	Blue-lt.
978	○	322	Navy Blue-vy. lt.
147	✕	312	Navy Blue-lt.
149	●	336	Navy Blue

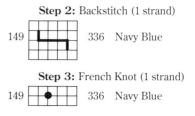

Step 2: Backstitch (1 strand)

Anchor	DMC	Color
149	336	Navy Blue

Step 3: French Knot (1 strand)

Anchor	DMC	Color
149	336	Navy Blue

Basket of Flowers

Stitched on crystal white Damask Aida 14, the finished design size is 6¼" x 4¾". The fabric was cut 13" x 11". See graph on page 16. See photo on page 13.

Fabric	Design Size
Aida 11	7⅞" x 6⅛"
Aida 18	4⅞" x 3¾"
Hardanger	4" x 3"

Anchor **DMC (used for sample)**

Step 1: Cross-stitch (2 strands)

Anchor	Symbol	DMC	Color
158	·	775	Baby Blue-vy. lt.
167	|	519	Sky Blue
160	–	813	Blue-lt.
130	□	809	Delft
131	∴	798	Delft-dk.
978	/	322	Navy Blue-vy. lt.
147	○	312	Navy Blue-lt.
150	●	823	Navy Blue-dk.
133	▲	796	Royal Blue-dk.
840	△	3768	Slate Green-dk.
399	✕	452	Shell Gray-med.

Step 2: Backstitch (1 strand)

Anchor	DMC	Color
150	823	Navy Blue-dk.

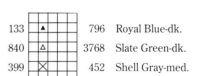

Ribbon Rosette Construction

1. Cut a 5" length of 4mm silk ribbon. Mark the center of the length of ribbon. Beginning at one end, fold end forward at right angle. Holding vertical length, begin rolling ribbon at fold horizontally to form bud.

2. Then, fold horizontal ribbon backward at right angle and continue rolling bud, aligning top edges of bud to second fold (rounding corner).

3. Continue folding ribbon backward at right angles and rolling bud to center mark. Secure, leaving needle and thread attached.

4. Stitch running thread on edge of remaining ribbon length. Gather tightly. Wrap gathered ribbon around bud. Secure and fluff flower.

5. Glue rosettes as desired on top of cross-stitch design.

Rosette Diagram

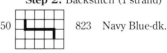

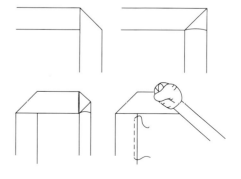

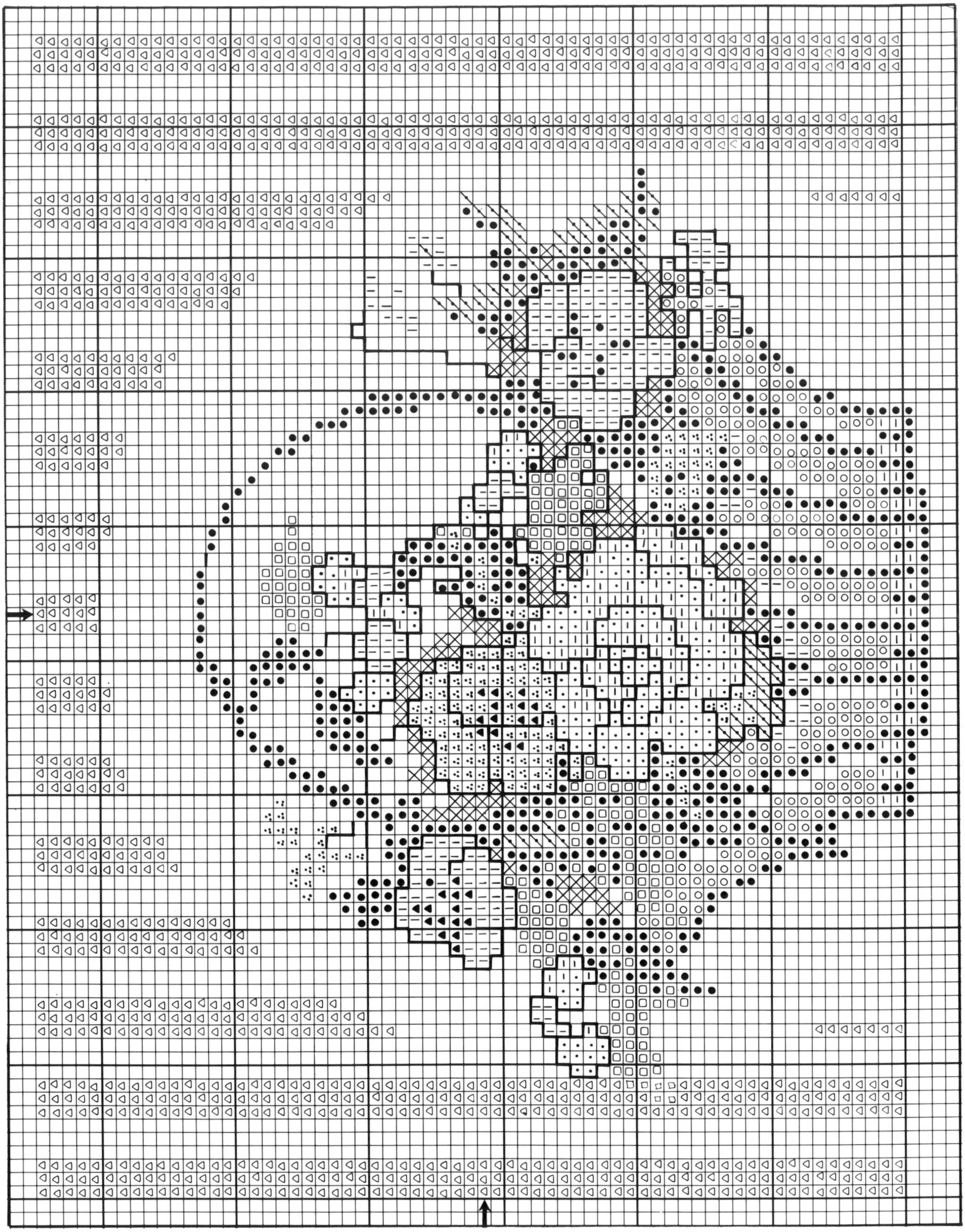

Basket of Flowers (Top) **Stitch count: 87 x 67**

Sweet Dreams

Stitched on white Murano 30 over 2 threads, the finished design size is 3⅝" x 4⅛" for one motif. The fabric was cut 25" x 11". See photo on page 17.

Fabric	Design Size
Aida 11	5" x 5½"
Aida 14	3⅞" x 4⅜"
Aida 18	3" x 3⅜"
Hardanger	2½" x 2¾"

Sweet Dreams Pillowcase

Materials
Finished design centered and
    trimmed to 22" x 8"
3 pieces of white Murano 30, each
    cut 22" x 8"
1 yd. of textured fabric for
    pillowcase
Two ⅝" buttons
Matching thread

Directions
All seams are ½".

1. Cut one 28" x 45" piece of textured fabric for pillowcase.

2. Cut two 16½" x 2¼" strips for tabs. With right sides facing, sew around, leaving one end open. Turn and press. Repeat for second tab. When finished, your tab should be 16" x 1⅛". Center button hole lengthwise on each tab. Set aside.

3. Place stitched design piece and one piece of white Murano 30 with right sides together. Stitch along bottom. Lay remaining two pieces of Murano 30 with right sides together and stitch along bottom. Place both pieces, right sides together, and stitch up sides. Turn and fold bottom portion under, forming a cuff. Press.

4. Fold textured fabric in half, with right sides together and matching 28" sides. Sew along side and top of pillowcase.

5. Pin tabs to back of pillowcase 7¼" from each side. Place cuff over end of pillowcase with right sides facing. Pin in place.

6. Check to make sure tabs will wrap from back to front and button. Adjust as necessary.

7. Sew through all layers, attaching cuff and tabs to pillowcase. Press seam toward bottom of pillowcase.

8. Finish off raw edges with a zigzag or a blanket stitch.

Anchor		DMC (used for sample)	
Step 1: Cross-stitch (2 strands)			
128	–	800	Delft-pale
145	O ⁄	334	Baby Blue-med.
118	●	340	Blue Violet-med.
Step 2: Backstitch (1 strand)			
145	⌐	334	Baby Blue-med. (on repeat)

Step 3: Mill Hill Glass Beads

⋮ 02026 Crystal Blue

Sweet Dreams (Top) **Stitch count: 55 x 61 (one motif)**

Floral Sampler

Stitched on white Belfast linen 32 over 2 threads, the finished design size is 7¾" x 10". The fabric was cut 14" x 16". Graph begins on page 22.

Fabric	Design Size
Aida 11	11⅜" x 14½"
Aida 14	8⅞" x 11⅜"
Aida 18	7" x 8⅞"
Hardanger	5⅝" x 7¼"

Anchor   **DMC (used for sample)**

Step 1: Cross-stitch (2 strands)

Anchor		DMC	
159	ǀ	3325	Baby Blue-lt.
130	–	809	Delft
145	○	334	Baby Blue-med.
161	□	826	Blue-med.
131	∴	798	Delft-dk.
978	△	322	Navy Blue-vy. lt.
170	●	3765	Peacock Blue-vy. dk.
816	▲	3750	Antique Blue-vy. dk.
117	▽	341	Blue Violet-lt.

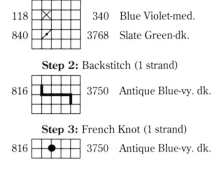

118	✕	340	Blue Violet-med.
840	╱	3768	Slate Green-dk.

Step 2: Backstitch (1 strand)

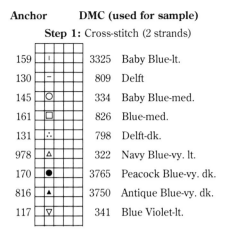

816		3750	Antique Blue-vy. dk.

Step 3: French Knot (1 strand)

816	●	3750	Antique Blue-vy. dk.

Floral Sampler (Top Left) **Stitch count: 125 x 159**

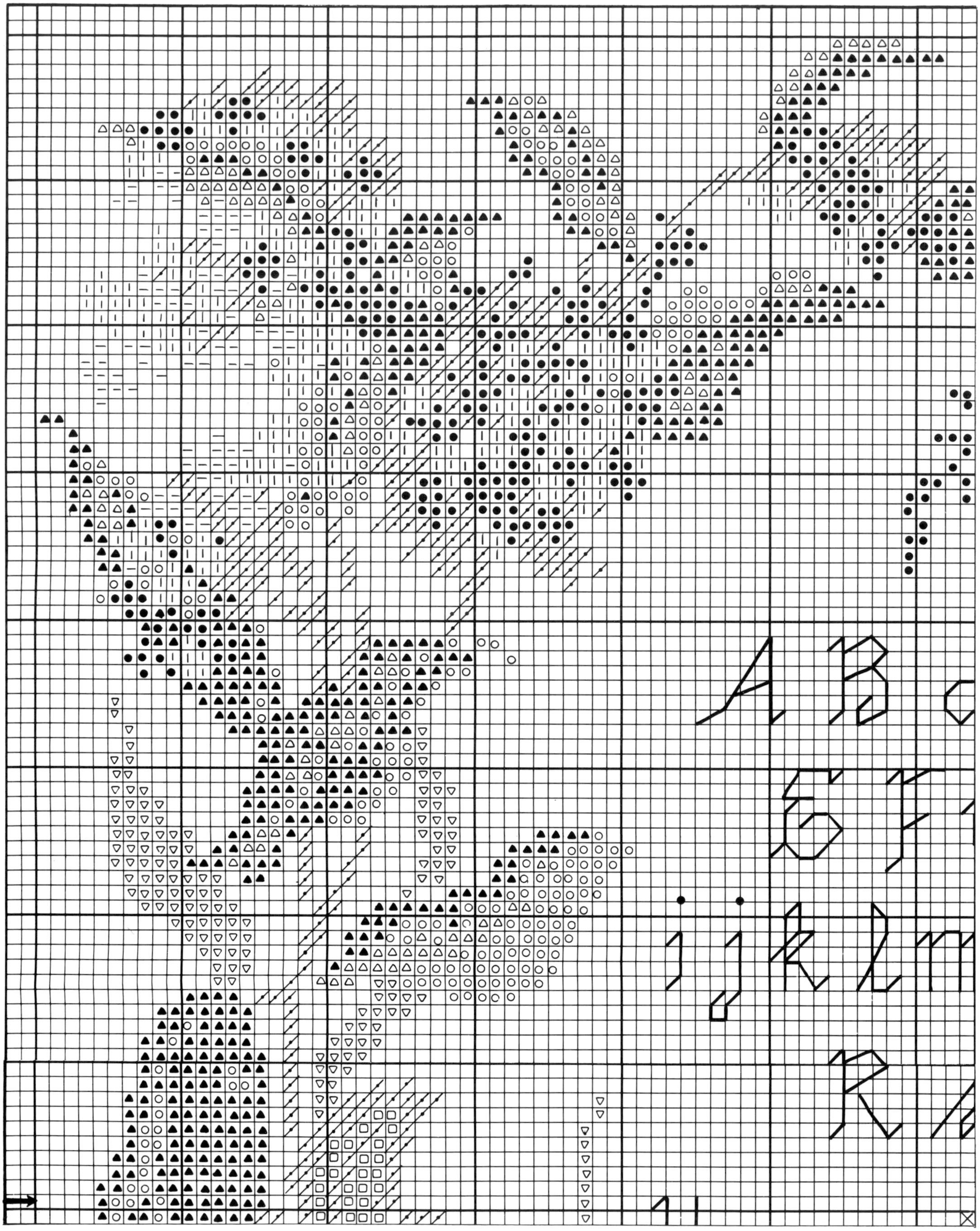

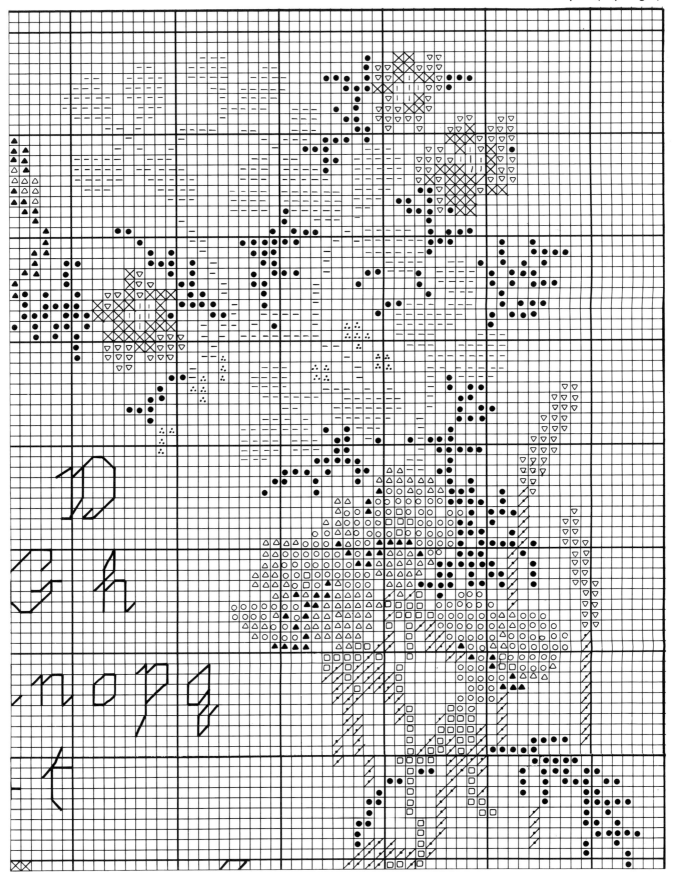

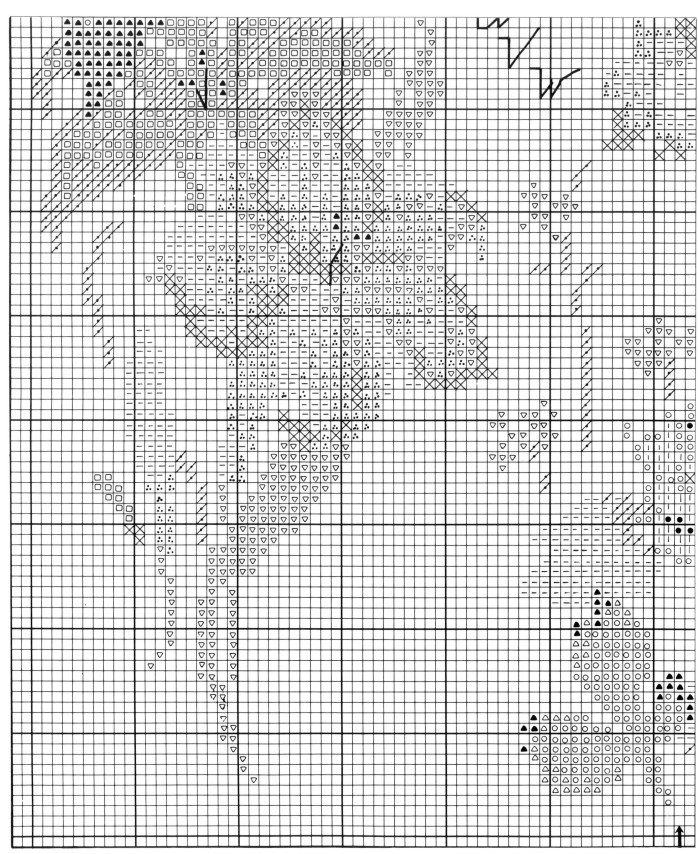

Floral Sampler (Bottom Left)

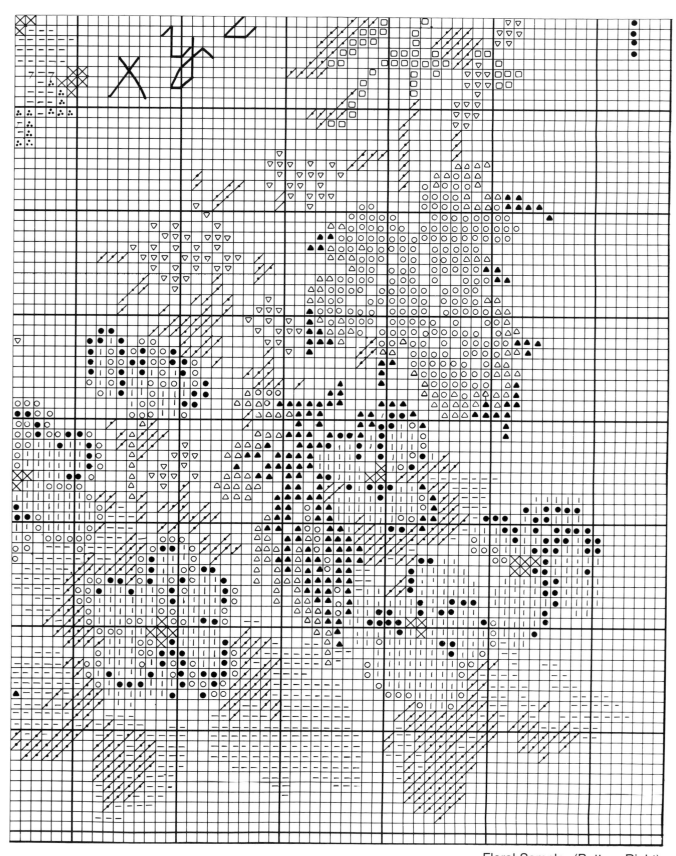

Floral Sampler (Bottom Right)

Wedgewood Plate

Stitched on white Annebelle 28 over 2 threads, the finished design size is 5⅜" x 5¾". The fabric was cut 12" x 12". See page 28 for **Wedgewood Plate Pillow**.

Fabric	Design Size
Aida 11	6⅞" x 6⅞"
Aida 18	4⅛" x 4⅛"
Hardanger	3⅜" x 3⅜"

Anchor		DMC (used for sample)	
		Step 1: Cross-stitch (2 strands)	
158	-	775	Baby Blue-vy. lt.
154	O	3755	Baby Blue
130	□	809	Delft
978	∴	322	Navy Blue-vy. lt.
131	X	798	Delft-dk.
149	●	311	Navy Blue-med.
118	△	340	Blue Violet-med.
849	·	927	Slate Green-med.

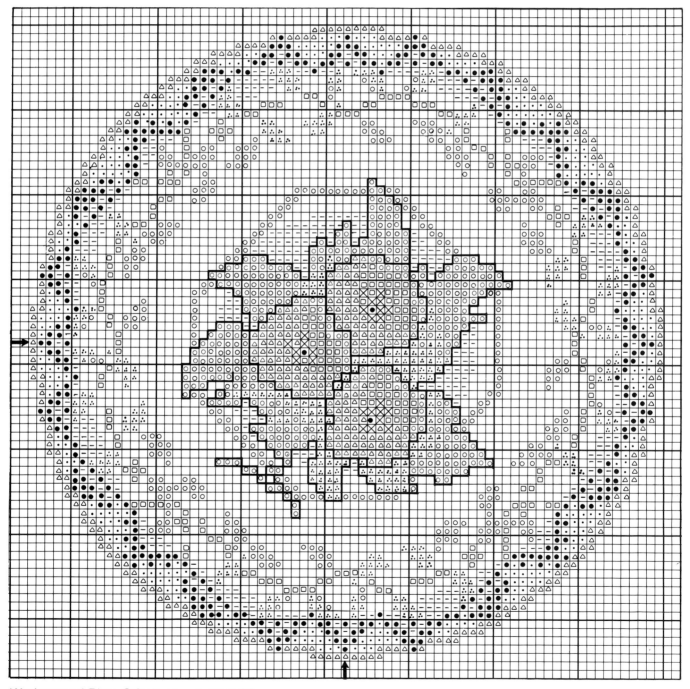

Wedgewood Plate **Stitch count: 75 x 75**

Delft Plate

Stitched on white Murano 30 over 2 threads, the finished design size is 5⅞" x 5⅞". The fabric was cut 12" x 12". See photo on Introduction page.

Fabric	Design Size
Aida 11	8⅛" x 8⅛"
Aida 14	6⅜" x 6⅜"
Aida 18	5" x 5"
Hardanger	4" x 4"

Anchor		DMC (used for sample)	
Step 1: Cross-stitch (2 strands)			
117	△	341	Blue Violet-lt.
940	O	3807	Cornflower Blue
159	·	3325	Baby Blue-lt.
145	−	334	Baby Blue-med.
147	●	312	Navy Blue-lt.
397	X	762	Pearl Gray-vy. lt.
Step 2: Backstitch (1 strand)			
147		312	Navy Blue-lt.

Delft Plate Pillow

Materials
Finished design trimmed to a 7½" circle
9" round pillow form
⅔ yd. blue satin; matching thread
Heavyweight thread
18" matching narrow cording
1½" covered button kit

Directions
1. From satin, cut 2 pieces measuring 10" x 45" each. Seam together along both short ends, forming a circle. Lay a length of heavyweight thread along one edge and sew a wide zigzag stitch over thread. Press opposite edge under ½".

2. Pull both ends of thread, gathering satin to fit around cross-stitched circle. Pin satin to cross-stitch with right sides together, adjusting gathers as you go. Hand-baste in place and check placement. Machine-stitch.

3. Tack cording around design edge to cover seam.

4. With heavy thread, run a gathering thread through fold along other edge of satin. Insert pillow form and pull threads tightly. Tie off.

5. Cover button according to manufacturer's instructions and sew to back center of pillow.

Wedgewood Plate Pillow
(from page 27)

Materials
Finished design centered and trimmed to a 8" circle
12" round purchased pillow (ours is blue velvet with tassels)
Matching thread
5" circle of fleece
5" circle of cardboard

Directions
Sew a basting stitch around edge of design circle. Layer as follows: cardboard, fleece and stitching, right side up. Pull gathering thread tightly and knot off end. Place on top of pillow and pin in place. Hand-sew to pillow.

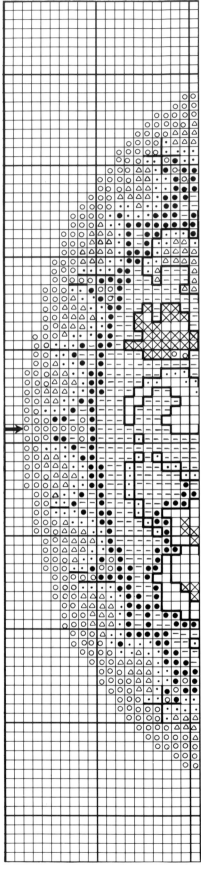

Delft Plate (Left)
Stitch count: 89 x 89

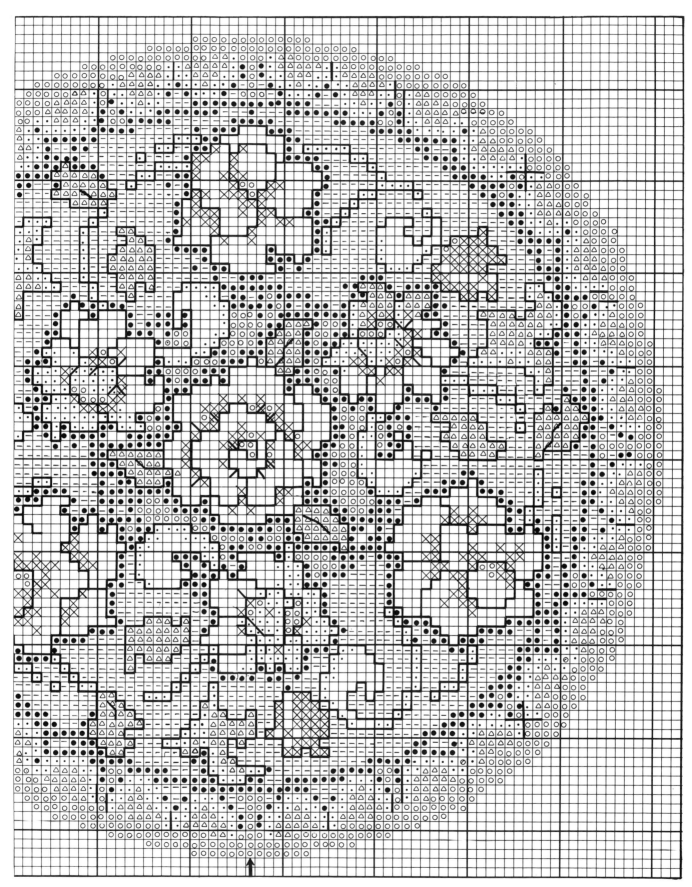

Delft Plate (Right)

Garden Song

Stitched on French Lace linen 28 over 2 threads, the finished design size is 5¾" x 8". The fabric was cut 12" x 14".

Fabric	Design Size
Aida 11	7⅜" x 10⅛"
Aida 18	4½" x 6¼"
Hardanger	3⅝" x 5⅛"

Anchor		DMC	(used for sample)

Step 1: Cross-stitch (2 strands)

1	+		White
926	/ /		Ecru
343	– /	3752	Antique Blue-ultra vy. lt.
130	△	809	Delft
118	● /	340	Blue Violet-med.
160	·	813	Blue-lt.
161	▲ /	826	Blue-med.
149	○	311	Navy Blue-med.
158	□	828	Blue-ultra vy. lt.
167	✕ /	3766	Peacock Blue-lt.
170	■	3765	Peacock Blue-vy. dk.
900	∴ /	3024	Brown Gray-vy. lt.
397	U /	762	Pearl Gray-vy. lt.

Step 2: Long Loose Stitch (1 strand)

149		311	Navy Blue-med. (harp strings)

Step 3: Backstitch (1 strand)

149		311	Navy Blue-med.

Step 4: French Knot (1 strand)

149	●	311	Navy Blue-med.

Garden Song (Top) **Stitch count: 80 x 112**

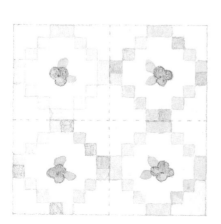

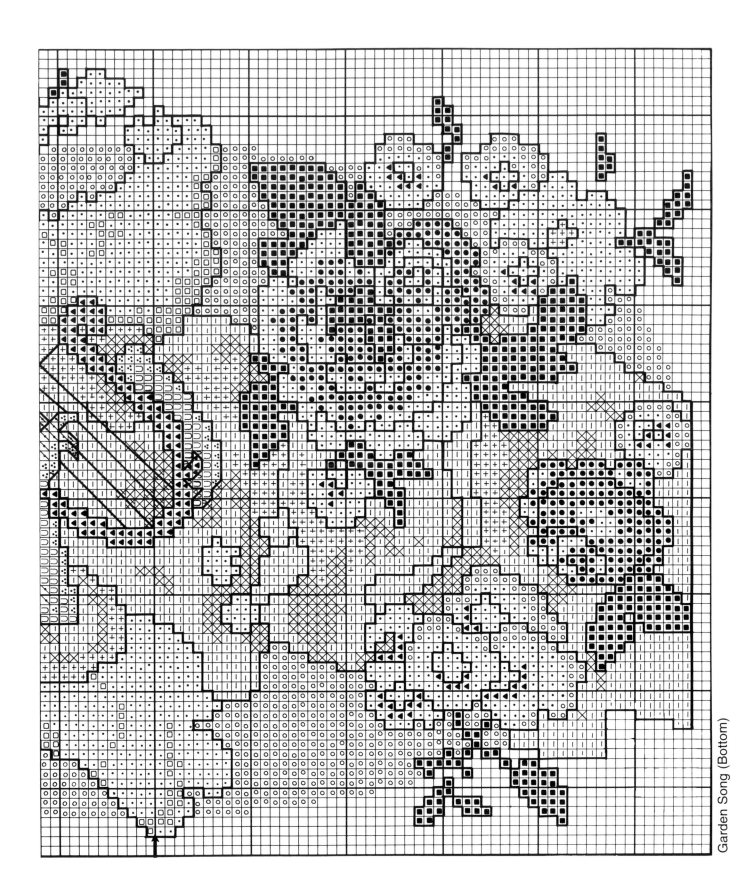

Garden Song (Bottom)

Classic Cherub

Stitched on white Cashel linen 28 over 2 threads, the finished design size is 6½" x 4⅞". The fabric was cut 14" x 12". See photo on page 33.

Fabric	Design Size
Aida 11	8¼" x 6¼"
Aida 18	5" x 3⅞"
Hardanger	4⅛" x 3⅛"

Classic Cherub Pillow

Materials
Finished design trimmed to
    9" x 10"
½ yd. crushed navy velvet cut into
    5 pieces:
      Two 4" x 15" pieces
      Two 4" x 10½" pieces
      16" x 15" piece
2 yds. braided cording
Seventy 1½"-long silver bugle
    beads
Seventy ⅜" round silver ball beads
Seventy 1/16" blue seed beads
Beading needle and matching
    beading thread
Heavy thread to punch corners
Stuffing

Directions
All seams are ½".

1. Sew strips around pillow top with short pieces matching the top and bottom of the design fabric and long pieces matching sides. Press seams.

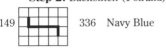
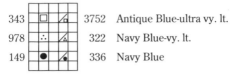

Anchor		DMC (used for sample)	
Step 1: Cross-stitch (2 strands)			
343		3752	Antique Blue-ultra vy. lt.
978		322	Navy Blue-vy. lt.
149		336	Navy Blue
Step 2: Backstitch (1 strand)			
149		336	Navy Blue

2. With right sides together, sew front piece to back of pillow, leaving a 5" opening at the bottom center for turning and stuffing.

3. Using heavy thread, sew a basting stitch across each corner 1¾" in from corner and pull tightly. Wrap thread around to secure. Knot and tie off. This will bunch up the corners when you stuff your pillow. Turn pillow right side out.

4. Stuff pillow firmly. Whipstitch the opening closed. Stitch braid to edge of pillow on seam, easing as needed around corners. Attach beads to braid as desired. Stitch through a long bugle bead, a round silver ball bead, and through a blue seed bead. Then come up through the round silver ball bead, the long bugle bead and through the braid.

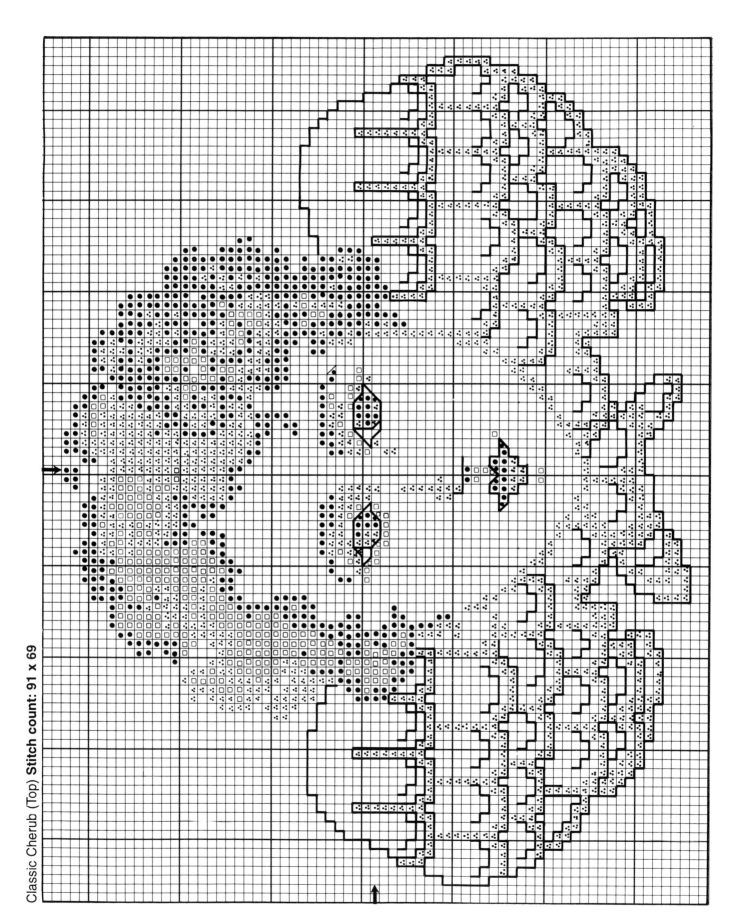

Classic Cherub (Top) **Stitch count: 91 x 69**

Afternoon Mosaic

Stitched on white Glasgow linen 28 over 2 threads, the finished design size is 8⅝" x 8⅝". The fabric was cut 15" x 15".

Fabric	Design Size
Aida 11	10⅞" x 10⅞"
Aida 18	6⅝" x 6⅝"
Hardanger	5½" x 5½"

Anchor		DMC (used for sample)	
Step 1: Cross-stitch (2 strands)			
158		3756	Baby Blue-ultra vy. lt.
975		3753	Antique Blue-vy. lt.
160		3761	Sky Blue-lt.
167		3766	Peacock Blue-lt.
117		341	Blue Violet-lt.
940		3807	Cornflower Blue
130		809	Delft

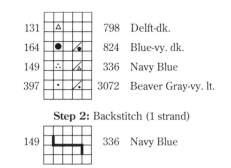

Anchor		DMC	
131		798	Delft-dk.
164		824	Blue-vy. dk.
149		336	Navy Blue
397		3072	Beaver Gray-vy. lt.
Step 2: Backstitch (1 strand)			
149		336	Navy Blue

Afternoon Mosaic (Top Left) **Stitch count: 120 x 120**

Afternoon Mosaic (Top Right)

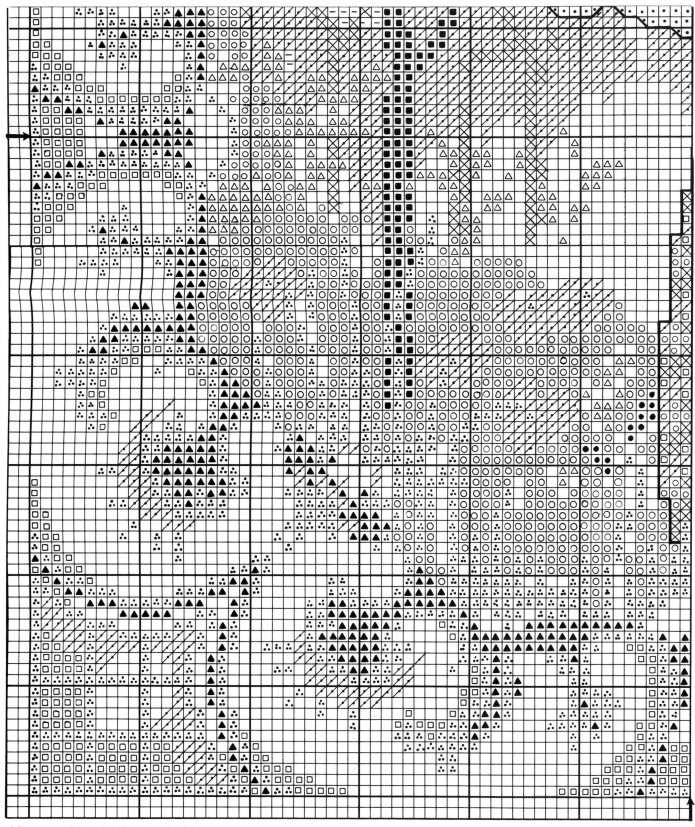

Afternoon Mosaic (Bottom Left)

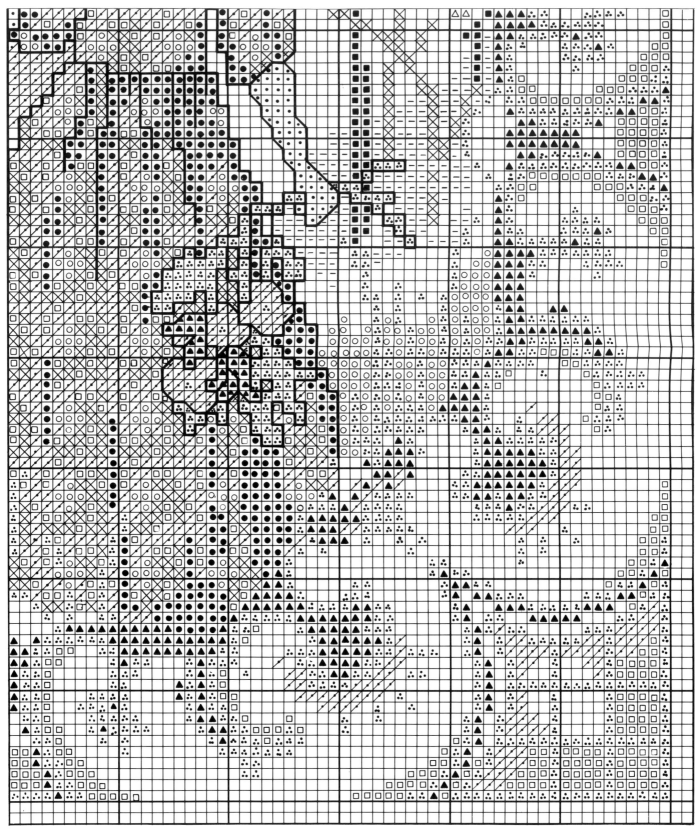

Afternoon Mosaic (Bottom Right)

Bath Time Trio Washcloth

Stitched on white Aida 14, the finished design size for one motif is 2⅜" x 1¼". The fabric was cut 13" x 4" for a completed washcloth.

Fabric	Design Size
Aida 11	3⅛" x 1½"
Aida 18	1⅞" x 1"
Hardanger	1½" x ¾"

Bath Time Trio Hand Towel

Stitched on white Aida 14, the finished design size for one motif is 2⅝" x 1⅞". The fabric was cut 15" x 4" for a completed towel.

Fabric	Design Size
Aida 11	3⅜" x 2½"
Aida 18	2" x 1½"
Hardanger	1⅝" x 1¼"

Bath Time Trio Bath Towel

Stitched on white Aida 14, the finished design size for one motif is 2⅞" x 2⅝". The fabric was cut 23" x 5" for a completed towel.

Fabric	Design Size
Aida 11	3¾" x 3¼"
Aida 18	2¼" x 2"
Hardanger	1⅞" x 1⅝"

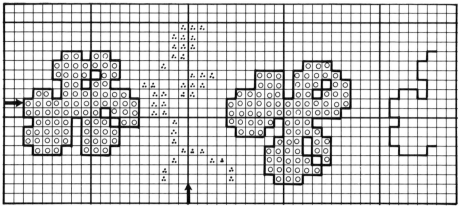

Bath Time Trio Washcloth **Stitch count: 34 x 17 (one motif)**

Bath Time Trio Washcloth

Anchor		DMC (used for sample)	
Step 1: Cross-stitch (2 strands)			
168	O	518	Wedgewood-lt.
117	∴	341	Blue Violet-lt.
Step 2: Backstitch (1 strand)			
162		517	Wedgewood-dk.

Bath Time Trio Hand Towel

Anchor			DMC (used for sample)	
Step 1: Cross-stitch (2 strands)				
167	O		519	Sky Blue
168	△	◹	518	Wedgewood-lt.
162	▲	◹	517	Wedgewood-dk.
117	✕		341	Blue Violet-lt.
Step 2: Backstitch (1 strand)				
162			517	Wedgewood-dk.

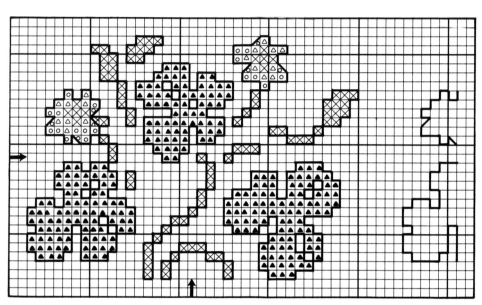

Bath Time Trio Hand Towel **Stitch count: 37 x 27 (one motif)**

Bath Time Trio Bath Towel

Anchor			DMC (used for sample)	
Step 1: Cross-stitch (2 strands)				
167	O		519	Sky Blue
168	△	◹	518	Wedgewood-lt.
162	▲	◹	517	Wedgewood-dk.
117	✕		341	Blue Violet-lt.
Step 2: Backstitch (1 strand)				
162			517	Wedgewood-dk.

Bath Time Trio Bath Towel **Stitch count: 41 x 36 (one motif)**

Ring o' Roses

Stitched on French lace linen 28 over 2 threads, the finished design size is 4¼" x 4¼" (one fourth of the completed design). The fabric for the complete piece was cut 15" x 15".

Fabric	Design Size
Aida 11	5½" x 5½"
Aida 18	3⅜" x 3⅜"
Hardanger	2¾" x 2¾"

To complete the framed piece, stitch design, turn this page one-quarter turn clockwise and stitch again, adding on to the right of the piece. Repeat two more turns until square is completed.

Anchor		DMC (used for sample)	

Step 1: Cross-stitch (2 strands)

387	·	712	Cream
158	+	747	Sky Blue-vy. lt.
167	∴	3766	Peacock Blue-lt.
161	╱	3760	Wedgewood-med.
131	□	798	Delft-dk.

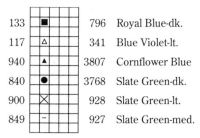

133	■	796	Royal Blue-dk.
117	△	341	Blue Violet-lt.
940	▲	3807	Cornflower Blue
840	●	3768	Slate Green-dk.
900	✕	928	Slate Green-lt.
849	–	927	Slate Green-med.

Step 2: Backstitch (1 strand)

127	└	939	Navy Blue-vy. dk.

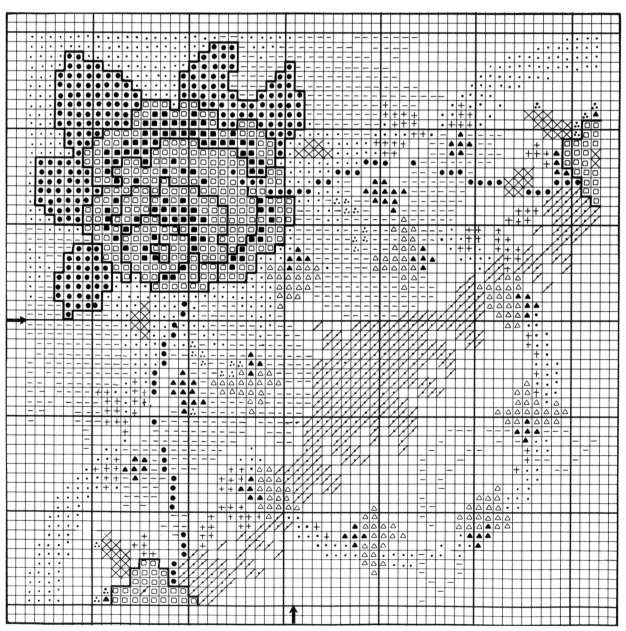

Ring o' Roses **Stitch count for one-fourth of design: 60 x 60**

Debra Wells

My lifelong love of the arts has found its way to cross-stitch design. I am a legal secretary in a prosecutor's office and spend my free hours designing and stitching cross-stitch patterns. My home is in Ogden, Utah, with my husband, Larry, and my son, Eli.

I was born in Laramie, Wyoming, in 1954 and inherited most of my talent from my mother, Mary, who is a talented designer and seamstress. Raising my sister and me as a single mother, she made our clothes herself and taught us to think creatively. Originally, this was her way of entertaining and clothing us inexpensively. But what began as a necessity grew into a lifelong love of working together to create not only the necessities, but objects of beauty with our hands and imaginations.

Fond memories of working with homemade salt clay (smelling faintly of vinegar from being kept in leftover pickle jars) and helping design and create our handmade school clothes remain with me to this day. Mom always praised our efforts and taught us to challenge our creativity. She taught us that nothing was impossible if we really wanted it to happen and inspired us with her talent and skill. That inspiration and encouragement is still paramount in my work. When I talk to her about a particular design or construction problem, she is always ready with suggestions, wisdom and encouragement. As a result, my response to most things that I see is "We can make it." I've said that so many times that my son just laughs at me now. But it really is true. If you want to, you can create almost anything with your hands, your imagination and your heart.

Anything can be an inspiration for design, if you choose to see things from an artistic point of view: the simple twist of a vine of ivy or a potted plant, snow, mountains, the moonlight.

Barber lake pine

The open heart and home of an aunt of mine inspired me to design "Room in the Heart." My "Traditional Tile" design sprang from the same setting. "Cornflower and Thistle" was born out of my discovery from a botanical textbook that the lovely little blue cornflower and thorny old thistle are members of the same family.

My childhood love of fairies (I used to imagine that the sparkles of new snow in the winter sun were little fairies) and remembering a poem which began "There are fairies at the bottom of my garden" inspired the "Midnight Fairy" design. Anything and everything can be an inspiration, if you see with your heart and have the courage to try.

rocky point

Traditional Tile

Stitched on white Damask Aida 14, the finished design size is 4¾" x 5". The fabric was cut 9" x 9".

Fabric	Design Size
Aida 11	6¼" x 6⅜"
Aida 18	3¾" x 3⅞"
Hardanger	3" x 3⅛"

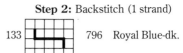

Anchor		DMC (used for sample)	
		Step 1: Cross-stitch (2 strands)	
145	△	334	Baby Blue-med.
130	□	809	Delft
130	○	799	Delft-med.
131	✕	798	Delft-dk.
133	●	796	Royal Blue-dk.

Step 2: Backstitch (1 strand)

133		796	Royal Blue-dk.

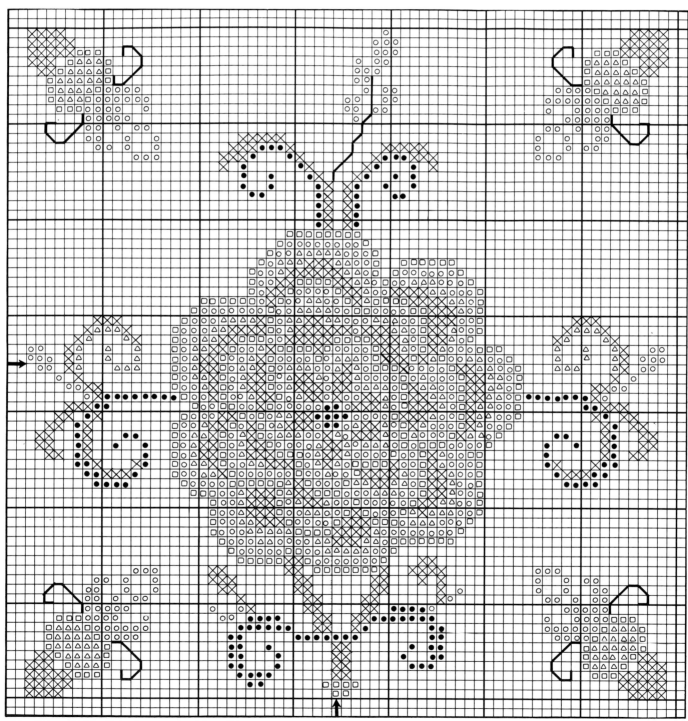

Traditional Tile **Stitch count: 67 x 70**

Midnight Fairy

Stitched on antique white Belfast
linen 32 over 2 threads, the finished
design size is 7½" x 9⅜". The fabric
was cut 14" x 16". Graph begins on
page 52.

Fabric	Design Size
Aida 11	10⅞" x 13¾"
Aida 14	8⅜" x 10¾"
Aida 18	6⅝" x 8⅜"
Hardanger	5½" x 6⅞"

Anchor		DMC (used for sample)	
Step 1: Cross-stitch (2 strands)			
1	+		White
975		3753	Antique Blue-vy. lt.
154	H	3755	Baby Blue
978		322	Navy Blue-vy. lt.
129	–	809	Delft
130	□	799	Delft-med.
131	■	798	Delft-dk.
167	/	3766	Peacock Blue-lt.
169	✕	806	Peacock Blue-dk.
170	●	3765	Peacock Blue-vy. dk.
922		930	Antique Blue-dk.
816	○	3750	Antique Blue-vy. dk.
150	◆	823	Navy Blue-dk.
158	ǀ	775	Baby Blue-vy. lt. (1 strand)
		001J	Silver Japan thread (1 strand)
158	▲	775	Baby Blue-vy. lt. (1 strand)
		001J	Silver Japan thread (1 strand)
159	△	3325	Baby Blue-lt. (1 strand)
		001J	Silver Japan thread (1 strand)
Step 2: Backstitch (1 strand)			
130		799	Delft-med. (wings)
150		823	Navy Blue-dk. (all else)
Step 3: Beads			
	◪	42024	Heather Mauve
	▲	42029	Tapestry Teal (sewn over cross-stitch)

Barber lake pine

Cornflower and Thistle

Stitched on white Murano 30 over 2 threads, the finished design size is 13⅜" x 11⅞". The fabric was cut 17" x 15". Graph begins on page 58.

Fabric	Design Size
Aida 11	18⅛" x 16⅛"
Aida 14	14¼" x 12¾"
Aida 18	11⅛" x 9⅞"
Hardanger	9⅛" x 8⅛"

Cornflower and Thistle Pillow

Materials
Finished design trimmed to within ½" of stitching
One 14" and one 3" blue fabric square; matching thread
Fancy button for front
1½" covered-button kit for back
Long needle
Small bag of stuffing

Directions
1. Trim the 14" fabric square to same size as design piece. Place both pieces right sides together and sew a ½" seam around edges, leaving a 4" opening. Turn, stuff and whipstitch closed.

2. Cover button with 3" fabric square following manufacturer's instructions. Using four strands of thread, start at back of pillow and stitch through center, attaching fancy button. Go back through to back of pillow and sew on covered button. Pull snugly and knot off.

Anchor		DMC	(used for sample)

Step 1: Cross-stitch (2 strands)

Anchor		DMC	
145	△	334	Baby Blue-med.
130	−	799	Delft-med.
131	□	798	Delft-dk.
940	∴	792	Cornflower Blue-dk.
132	╱	797	Royal Blue
133	●	796	Royal Blue-dk.
134	○	820	Royal Blue-vy. dk.

Step 2: Backstitch (1 strand)

Anchor		DMC	
134	▃	820	Royal Blue-vy. dk.

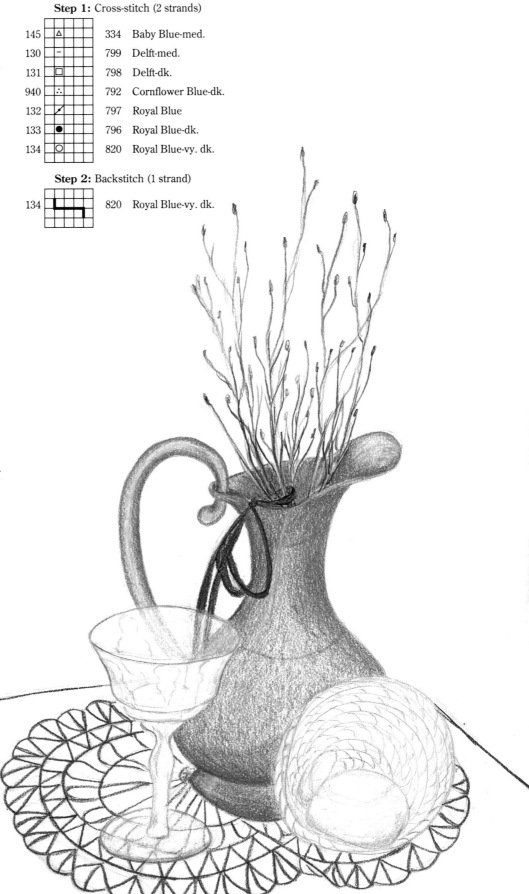

Begin to Weave

Stitched on white Murano 30 over 2 threads, the finished design size is 12⅞" x 7¼". The fabric was cut 19" x 14". Graph begins on page 66.

Fabric	Design Size
Aida 11	17⅝" x 9⅞"
Aida 14	13⅞" x 7¾"
Aida 18	10¾" x 6"
Hardanger	8⅞" x 4⅞"

Anchor		DMC (used for sample)	

Step 1: Cross-stitch (2 strands)

130	−	799	Delft-med.
131	△	798	Delft-dk.
132	○	797	Royal Blue
134	●	820	Royal Blue-vy. dk.

Step 2: Backstitch (1 strand)

130	└	799	Delft-med.

Begin to Weave Ribbon Directions

See **Ribbon Embroidery**

Instructions on page 141. Using 4mm silk ribbon, stitch design according to stitch diagram and stitch guide as follows:

	Ribbon	Stitch
1	Lt. blue silk	Spider Web Rose
2	Pale blue silk	Spider Web Rose
3	Pale blue silk	Stem Stitch
4	Pale blue silk	Japanese Ribbon
5	Pale blue silk	Curved Whipstitch
6	Pale blue silk	Couched Ribbon
7	Med. blue silk	Lazy Daisy
8	Med. blue silk	French Knot
9	Navy silk	French Knot
10	Navy silk	Lazy Daisy
11	Navy silk	Straight Stitch
12		Clear bead

Begin to Weave Stitch Diagram

194 × 108
aida 11 = 17⅝ × 9⅞
14 = 13⅞ × 7¾
18 = 10¾ × 6"

Begin to Weave (Top Left) **Stitch count: 194 x 108**

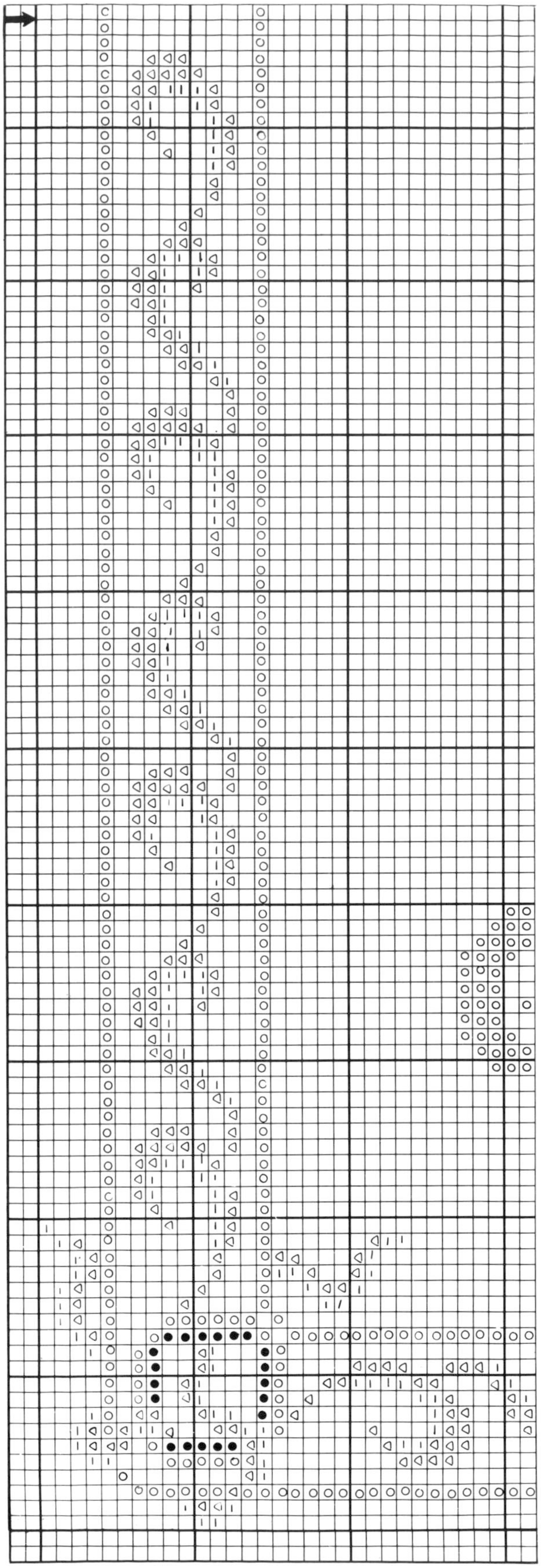

Begin to Weave (Top Right)

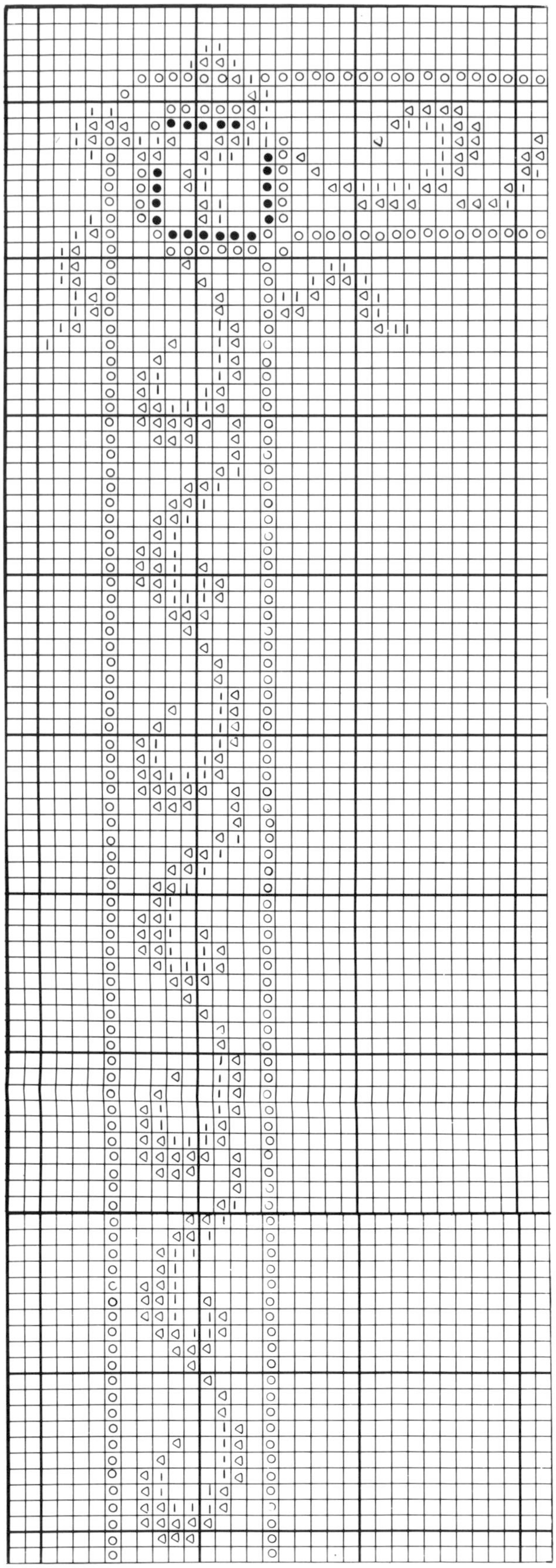

Begin to Weave (Bottom Left)

German Prayers

68

Antique Hearts

Stitched on white Belfast linen 32 over 2 threads, the finished design size for one motif is 4⅝" x 2". The fabric was cut 29" x 26".

Fabric	Design Size
Aida 11	6¾" x 3"
Aida 14	5¼" x 2¼"
Aida 18	4⅛" x 1¾"
Hardanger	3⅜" x 1½"

Anchor		DMC (used for sample)

Step 1: Cross-stitch (2 strands)

128	□	800	Delft-pale
130	╱	809	Delft
131	△	799	Delft-med.
132	○	797	Royal Blue
133	●	796	Royal Blue-dk.

Antique Hearts Napkin

Materials
Finished piece trimmed to 28" x 24"
    with design centered along
    bottom edge
2½" x 5" piece of white linen
White thread

Directions
1. Roll-hem all sides of design piece. Press.

2. Roll-hem long edges of small piece of linen. Bring short ends together with right side out and slip-stitch to bottom center of napkin.

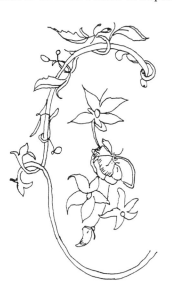

Antique Hearts (Top) **Stitch count: 74 x 32 (one motif)**

77

Royal Beaded Stocking

Stitched on antique white Cashel linen 28 over 2 threads, the finished design size for one motif is 2⅛" x 2¼". The fabric was cut 24" x 20" for the complete stocking cuff. The motif is repeated 11 times and stitched along the side of the cuff. The beaded emblem is stitched on white perforated plastic 14, the finished design is 2⅛" x 2¼". The perforated plastic was cut 6" x 6".

Fabric	Design Size
Aida 11	2⅝" x 3"
Aida 18	1⅝" x 1¾"
Hardanger	1⅜" x 1½"

Mill Hill (used for sample)

Step 1: Glass Beads

Symbol	Bead
/	00161 Crystal
△	02006 Ice Blue
○	00146 Lt. Blue
●	00020 Royal Blue

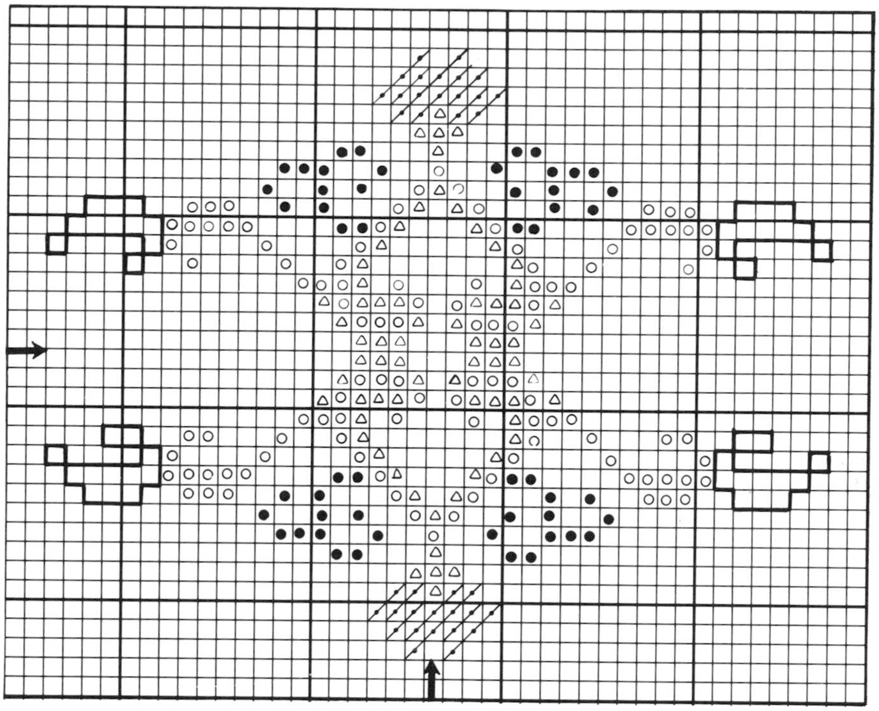

Royal Beaded Stocking **Stitch count: 29 x 32 (one motif)**

Royal Beaded Stocking Finishing

Materials

Purchased plastic or paper maché boot
Finished design trimmed to 22" x 18" (design will be stitched across center of lower half)
One individual finished design cut from plastic canvas
¾ yd. white velvet
Thread: white, lt. blue
1 yd. 2"-wide sheer white ribbon
½ yd. of 1/16" elastic
Lt. blue fabric dye
Tracing paper
Hot glue gun and glue sticks
Stapler

Directions

1. Dye white velvet according to manufacturer's instructions. Wring gently and lay flat. Let dry. Do not iron fabric, as crinkling adds finish.

2. Using patterns on page 80, enlarge 150 %. With right sides together, cut two stockings and one sole. With right sides facing, stitch stockings together along center front seam. Press seam open. Turn top long edge ¼" to wrong side and stitch. With right sides facing, stitch center back seam.

3. Fold sole piece in half lengthwise to find center; mark. With right sides facing, pin sole to bottom edge of stocking, matching center with seams. Beginning with heel, stitch pieces together. Turn.

4. Slide stocking onto plastic boot. Roll top of stocking into boot. Pull fabric tightly and staple back top of boot. Smooth fabric to front of boot and make a box pleat in center top of stocking. Staple. Measure 9½" down from center top, make a box pleat and tack. Smooth fabric up and finish stapling around top of boot.

5. To make cuff, bring 18" ends together with right sides facing. Stitch, forming a tube. Turn out halfway, bringing raw edges together and forming a cuff (design will be inside). Stitch around raw edge.

6. With seam in back, slide cuff down over boot until raw edge is 2½" from top. Tie elastic tightly around boot about 1" below raw edge. Pull cuff over elastic and tuck into boot.

7. From ribbon, make a bow with long tails. Hot-glue bow over pleat in center of boot. Cascade tails, tacking randomly. Hot-glue plastic canvas design to center of bow.

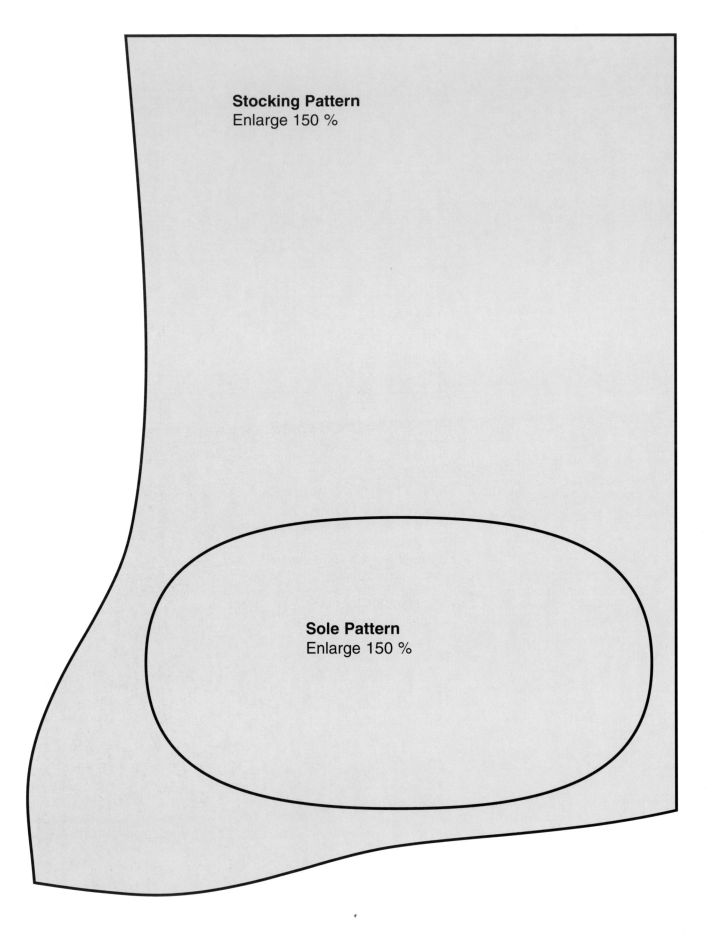

Stocking Pattern
Enlarge 150 %

Sole Pattern
Enlarge 150 %

Room in the Heart

Stitched on white Murano 30 over 2 threads, the finished design size is 8⅞" x 8⅝". The fabric was cut 15" x 15". See photo on page 81.

Fabric	Design Size
Aida 11	12⅛" x 11⅞"
Aida 14	9½" x 9¼"
Aida 18	7⅜" x 7¼"
Hardanger	6" x 5⅞"

Anchor		DMC (used for sample)	

Step 1: Cross-stitch (2 strands)

158		775	Baby Blue-vy. lt.
145		334	Baby Blue-med.
147		312	Navy Blue-lt.
150		823	Navy Blue-dk.

Step 2: Backstitch (1 strand)

150		823	Navy Blue-dk.

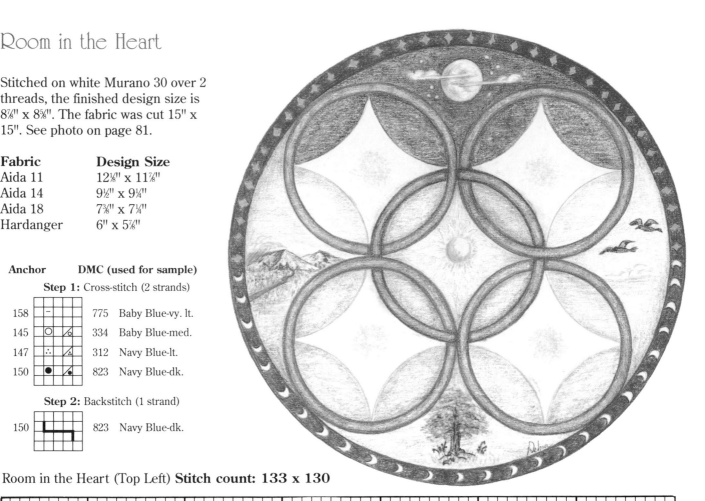

Room in the Heart (Top Left) **Stitch count: 133 x 130**

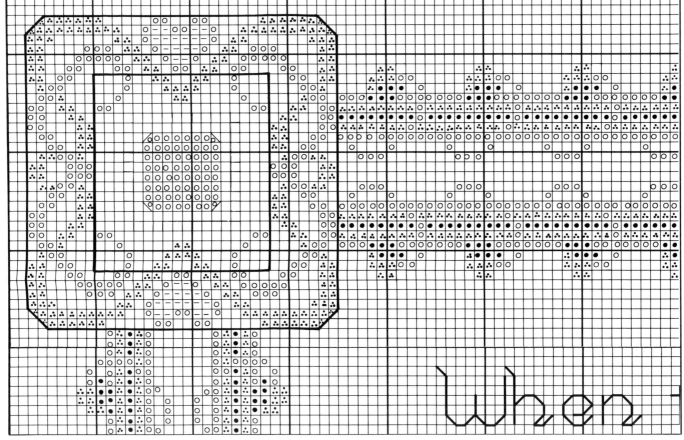

Room in the Heart (Top Right)

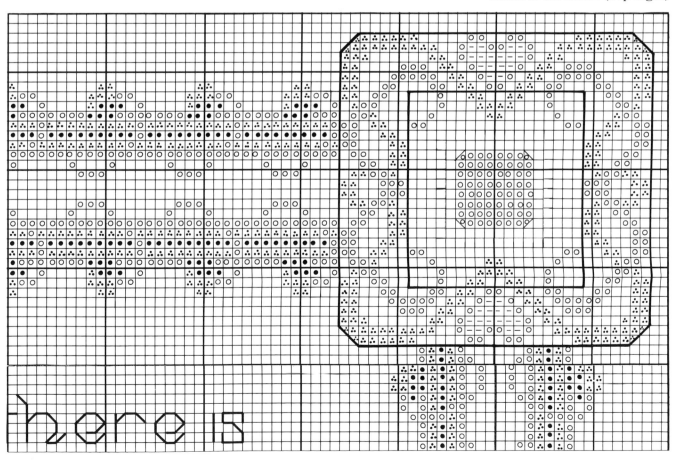

Netherlands Border

Stitched on white linen stitch band 22 over 2 threads, the finished design size for one motif is 3½" x 3¾". The fabric was cut 23" x 5".

Fabric	Design Size
Aida 14	2¾" x 3¾"
Aida 18	2⅛" x 2¼"
Hardanger	1¾" x 1⅞"

Anchor		DMC (used for sample)

Step 1: Cross-stitch (2 strands)

130	△	799	Delft-med.
131	O	798	Delft-dk.
978	□	322	Navy Blue-vy. lt.
133	●	796	Royal Blue-dk.

Netherlands Border Pillow Band

Materials
Finished design centered and trimmed to 20" long
Two 10" x 15½" pieces of blue print fabric; matching thread
Small bag stuffing

Directions
1. Place printed fabric right sides together and sew ½" seam around edge, leaving a 4" opening. Turn, stuff and whipstitch opening closed.

2. Bring ends of stitched piece right sides together and sew a seam, forming a band. Slip band over pillow.

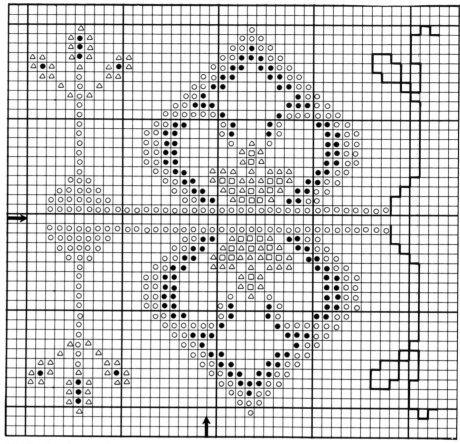

Netherlands Border **Stitch count: 38 x 41 (one motif)**

Gloria Judson

A fifth-generation Californian, I was born Gloria Anne Ewig in Palo Alto on Halloween, 1948. I attended Benjamin Cory Elementary School in San Jose before moving to Southern California, where my parents, Gordon and Ginnie Ewig, and my brother, Randy, and his family still reside.

Graduating from San Marino High School in 1966, I went on to U.C. Santa Barbara, where I became a Delta Gamma, a Little Sister of Minerva, saw Bo Diddley, banks burning, psychedelic sunsets and graduated with a B.A. in art history in 1970.

I began work as a stewardess for Pan American Airlines that summer, married in 1971 and bought a house in Manhattan Beach in 1972. After traveling to London, New Zealand, and Tahiti for several years, thanks to Pan Am, I got a job on the ground in the art department at Mattel Toys.

While there, I attended Art Center, College of Design, at night, which led to an incredible job at Northlight Studios in L.A., where I learned more than any school could have taught me about paste-up and production from Bob Garvin and by just being in the presence of some of the best illustrators in the business, including George Francuch, David Lindsay, and Tak Nakamura.

During the mid-seventies, I returned to college to get a teaching credential and taught junior high school in the South Bay area until my son, Grady, was born in 1978. My daughter, Hayley, was born in 1980 in the middle of major remodeling. I continued doing graphic design work and began doing residential interior decorating after the results of our beach remodel were published in a Los Angeles magazine back in the early eighties.

My parents will attest to the fact that I've been making posters and drawing houseplans on the living room floor forever...and I see no reason to stop this obsessive behavior now! I am presently living in Menlo Park as a single parent to a high school freshman, a sophomore, three big dogs and two little cats.

Opposite top right: Me on my graduation day with my brother, Randy, and my parents.
Top right: My cat, Hudson Judson.
Left: Clockwise from top are my Aunt Ann, my parents, Gordon and Ginnie Ewig, my son, Grady, my Uncle Gene, and my daughter, Hayley.

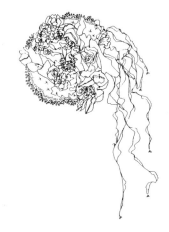

Quilt Block Houses

Stitched on white Murano 30 over 2 threads, the finished design size is 10⅞" x 6⅞". The fabric was cut 15" x 12".

Fabric	Design Size
Aida 11	14⅞" x 9½"
Aida 14	11¾" x 7⅜"
Aida 18	9⅛" x 5¾"
Hardanger	7½" x 4¾"

Anchor		DMC (used for sample)	
Step 1: Cross-stitch (2 strands)			
410		995	Electric Blue-dk.
134		820	Royal Blue-vy. dk.
127		939	Navy Blue-vy. dk.
Step 2: Backstitch (1 strand)			
134		820	Royal Blue-vy. dk.

Quilt Block Houses Pillow

Materials
Finished design trimmed to
   12½" x 9"
¼ yd. printed blue fabric; matching
   thread
½ yd. solid blue fabric
⅜ yd. muslin
24 oz. bag of stuffing
White marking pencil

Directions
All seams ½".

1. From muslin, cut two pieces measuring 12½" x16¼". With right sides together, sew around edges, leaving a 4" opening. Turn, press and stuff firmly. Whipstitch opening closed. Set aside; this will be your pillow form.

2. Cut four pieces of blue print fabric as follows: two 9" x 4½" and two 12½" x 4½". From solid blue fabric, cut four 4½" squares and one 19½" x 16" piece.

(continued on page 93)

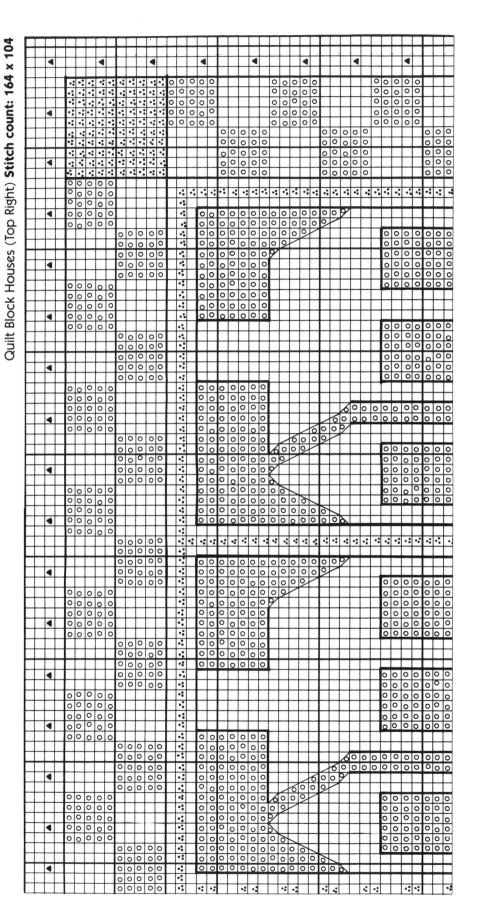

Quilt Block Houses (Top Right) **Stitch count: 164 x 104**

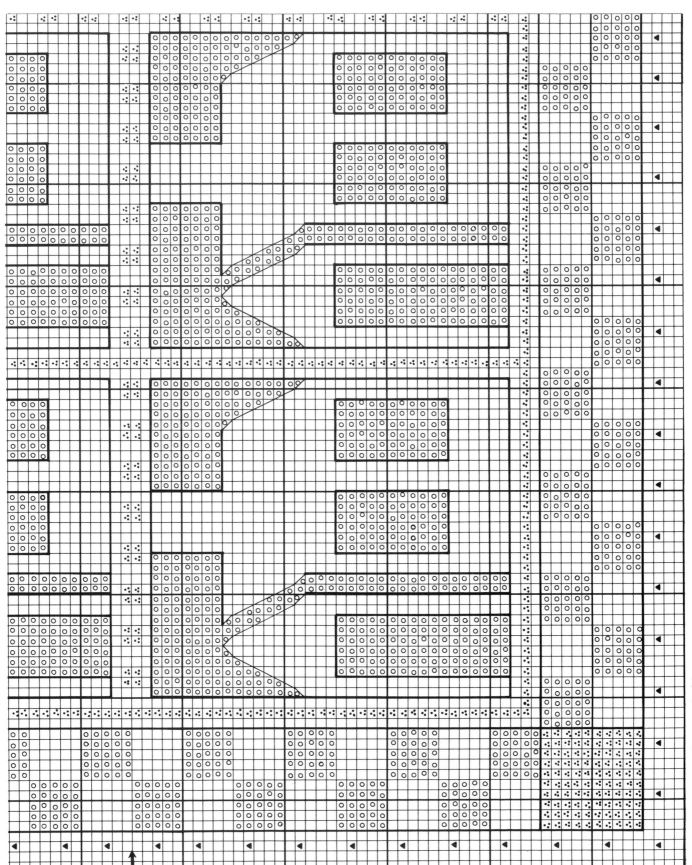

Quilt Block Houses (Bottom Left)

Ribbons and Roses

Stitched on white Cashel linen 28 over 2 threads, the finished design size is 6¾" x 4½". The fabric was cut 13" x 11". See graph on page 100.

Fabric	Design Size
Aida 11	8⅝" x 5¾"
Aida 18	5¼" x 3½"
Hardanger	4⅜" x 2⅞"

Anchor	Symbol	DMC (used for sample)	
Step 1: Cross-stitch (2 strands)			
975	•	3753	Antique Blue-vy. lt.
159	+	3325	Baby Blue-lt.
145	○	334	Baby Blue-med.
978	∴	322	Navy Blue-vy. lt.
164	●	824	Blue-vy. dk.
164	/	824	Blue-vy. dk.
816	−	3750	Antique Blue-vy. dk.
816	■	3750	Antique Blue-vy. dk.
185	△	964	Seagreen-lt.
188	X	943	Aquamarine-med.
189	▲	991	Aquamarine-dk.
Step 2: Backstitch (1 strand)			
150		823	Navy Blue-dk.
Step 3: Mill Hill Beads (sewn over cross-stitch)			
	/	00358	Cobalt Blue
	■	00146	Light Blue

Ribbons and Roses Ribbon Directions

See **Ribbon Embroidery Instructions** on page 141. Stitch design according to diagram below and stitch guide as follows:

Ribbon	Stitch
1 Med. blue silk—4mm	Spider Web Rose
2 Pale blue silk—4mm	Spider Web Rose
3 Powder blue silk—7mm	Spider Web Rose

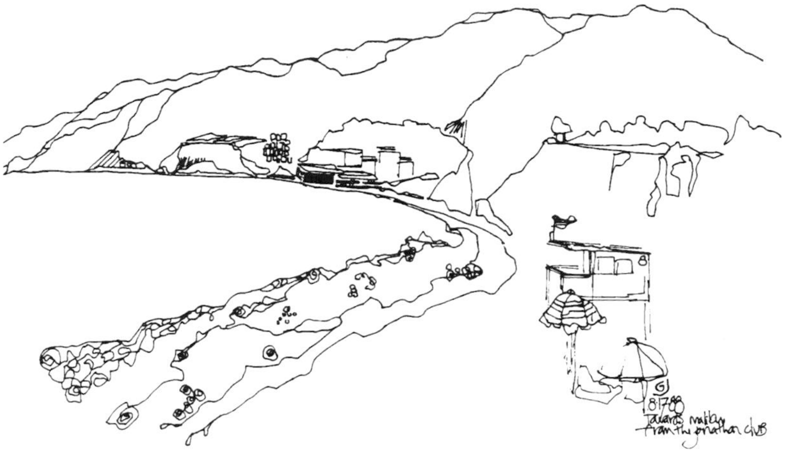

Ribbons and Roses Stitch Diagram

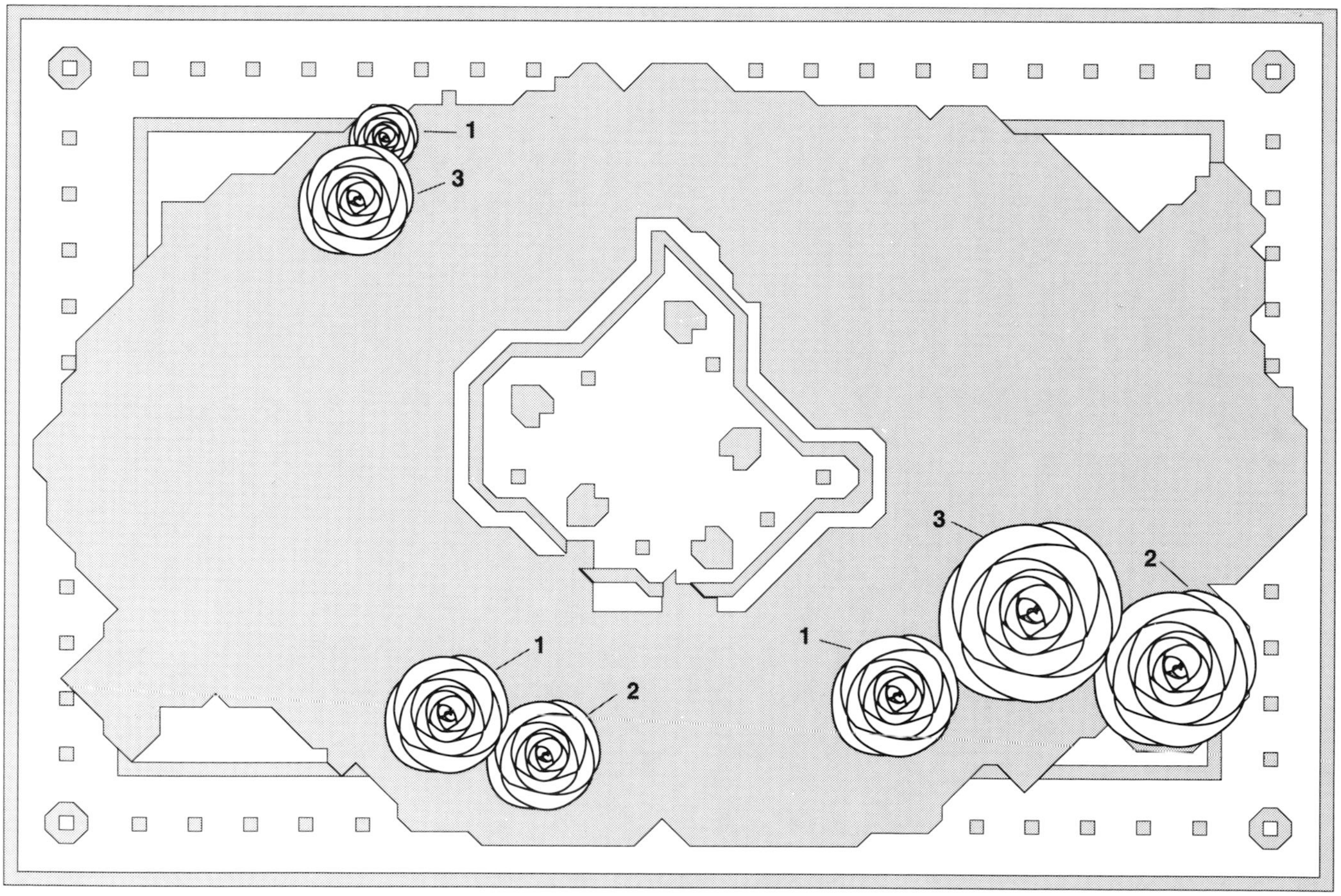

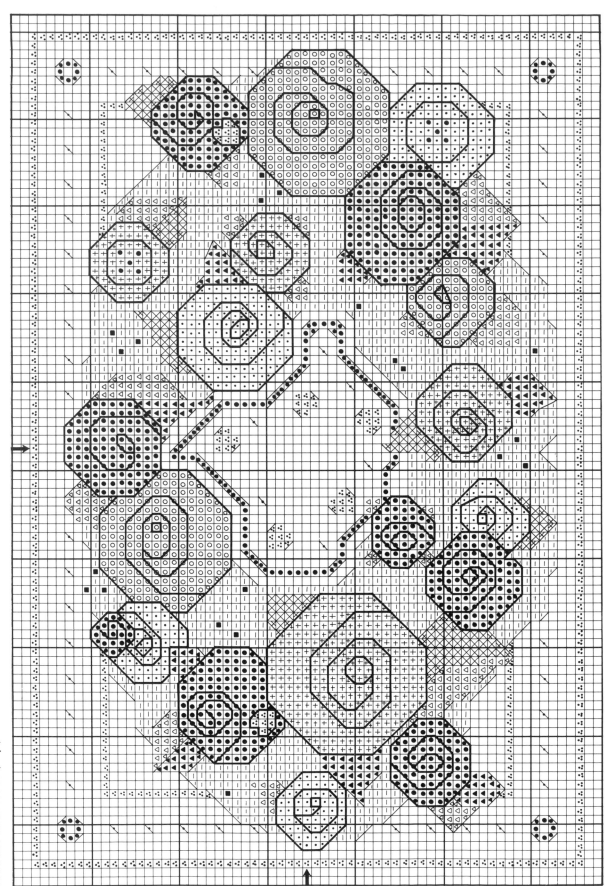

Ribbons and Roses (Top) **Stitch count: 95 x 63**

Blue Moon

Stitched on antique-blue Belfast linen 32 over 2 threads, the finished design size is 4" x 6⅛". The fabric was cut 10" x 13". See graph on page 106.

Fabric	Design Size
Aida 11	5¾" x 8⅞"
Aida 14	4⅝" x 7"
Aida 18	3½" x 5⅛"
Hardanger	2⅞" x 4½"

Materials
5" x 4" piece of cardboard
5" x 4" piece of fleece
5" x 4" piece of silver lamé
4mm silk embroidery ribbon:
    lt. blue, slate, royal, navy
4 assorted beads
46 lt. blue seed beads
26 dk. blue seed beads

Blue Moon Ribbon Directions
See **Ribbon Emboidery Instructions** on page 141. Using dressmaker's carbon, trace **Blue Moon Stitch Pattern** on page 110 to lamé. Stitch design according to diagram and stitch guide as follows:

	Ribbon	Stitch
1	Slate silk	Feather Stitch
2	Slate silk	Feather Stitch
3	Navy silk	Fly Stitch
4	Lt. blue silk	Fly Stitch
5	Lt. blue silk	Cretan Stitch
6	Royal blue silk	Cretan Stitch
7	Royal blue silk	Lazy Daisy
8	Navy silk	Lazy Daisy
9	Lt. blue silk	Lazy Daisy
10		Lt. blue bead
11		Dk. blue bead

Moon Assembly Directions
1. Using moon outline as pattern, cut one from cardboard. Cut fleece from pattern. Glue fleece to right side of cardboard.

2. Position finished design over fleece-covered moon and wrap. Whipstitch left edge of moon with lt. blue silk embroidery ribbon (number **12** on **Blue Moon Stitch Diagram**).

3. Cut a 7" length of navy silk embroidery ribbon and add assorted beads to tails. Fold ribbon near center and glue this point to the underside of moon according to the diagram.

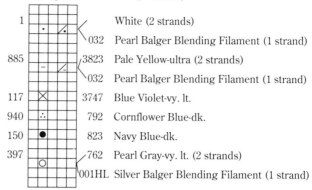

Anchor   DMC (used for sample)

Step 1: Cross-stitch (2 strands)

Anchor	Symbol	DMC	
1	· /		White (2 strands)
		032	Pearl Balger Blending Filament (1 strand)
885	– /	3823	Pale Yellow-ultra (2 strands)
		032	Pearl Balger Blending Filament (1 strand)
117	X	3747	Blue Violet-vy. lt.
940	∴	792	Cornflower Blue-dk.
150	●	823	Navy Blue-dk.
397		762	Pearl Gray-vy. lt. (2 strands)
	O	001HL	Silver Balger Blending Filament (1 strand)

Blue Moon Stitch Diagram

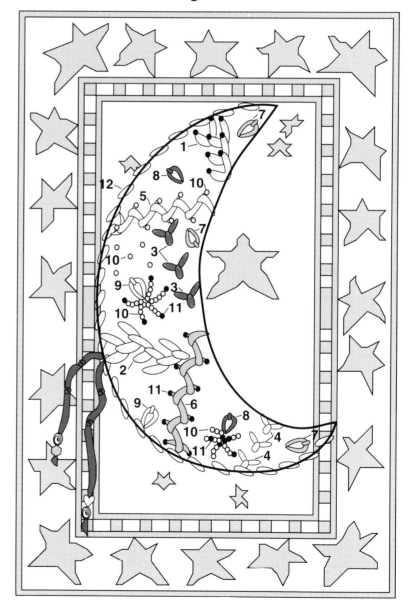

4. Sew or glue moon to cross-stitch design according to the diagram.

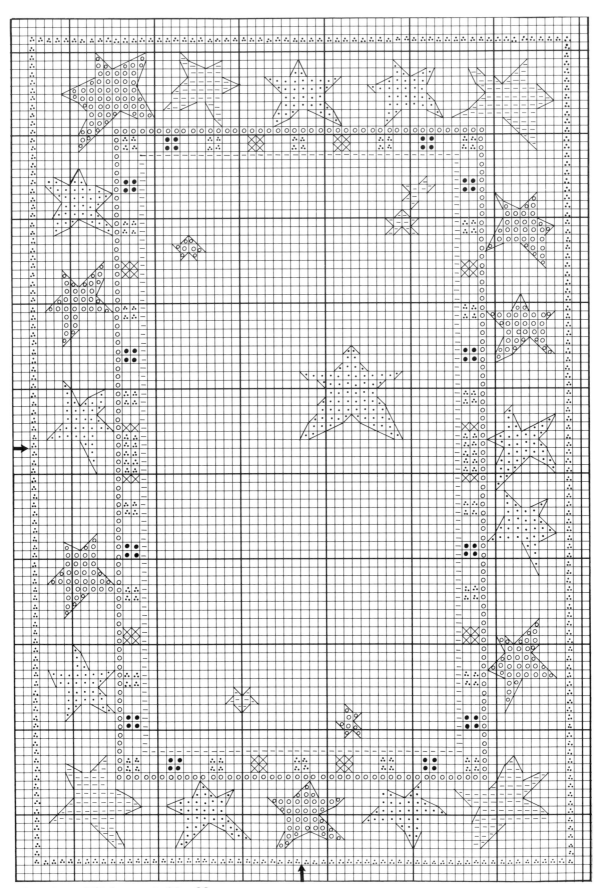

Blue Moon **Stitch count: 64 x 98**

Terrece Beesley

I was born and raised in Rexburg, Idaho. My family owned a large farm, raising wheat, barley and potatoes (of course). I have always loved my solitude and I am sure it comes from my childhood. I have four older brothers, lots of nieces and nephews, and we are a very close family.

My family farmed in the summer and skied all winter. I don't remember a Saturday or Sunday in the winter that wasn't spent on skis. So, I love the winter, but regret that I don't ski as much as I would like to these days.

The other sport I love is swimming, and anything that takes place in the water. I love to snorkel and scuba dive. My husband and I always plan our vacations around these activities. My husband's name is Jerry Poulson. This is the second marriage for both of us and we have five children between us, three boys and two girls—a real Brady bunch!

I love to read. My husband says I read everything that comes within fifty feet. My real passion is water-color. I try to work on my paintings as much as possible.

I keep a file cabinet full of photos, cards, pages torn from magazines, napkins, anything I see that interests me or might be of use later (artists call these "morgues"). When I start a design, I just sit down and start browsing through my files for a while, collecting ideas. I might end up with twenty possible ideas to use in a design. Then I start a series of very small sketches, working out the composition and values. When I am happy with that step, I'll enlarge my composition and put it on graph paper.

I'll usually work on a large design for a couple of days and then tack it to my bulletin board and start another piece. I have found that it is very important to back off and stare at a design for a couple of days. I can usually spot the problems if I leave it alone for a while. The time I spend "not drawing" is just as valuable as may drawing time. I like to work on several pieces at a time, so I can be drawing on one design while staring at another, and throwing together ideas for the third. Sometimes my walls are covered with "half-baked" artwork.

I love to manipulate color, playing warm colors against cool colors, and vivid colors against tones. I like to use many different variations of the same color in my designs—for instance, a periwinkle blue, a dull blue, a bright blue and a blue-green in the same piece. If I am shading an object, the highlights are always warmer, the shadows bluer and a bit duller. This approach gives my designs a lot of life and people seem to comment most on my use of color.

I work best when I am totally alone, although my children come and go and sometimes just sit and keep me company. I always listen to music when I am working—classical or rock music, depending on my mood and frustration level.

Momma's Little Angel

Stitched on white Murano 30 over 2 threads, the finished design size for one motif is 5½" x 1⅞". The fabric was cut 16" x 8" for one motif.

Fabric	Design Size
Aida 11	7½" x 2½"
Aida 14	5⅞" x 2"
Aida 18	4½" x 1½"
Hardanger	3¾" x 1¼"

Anchor			DMC (used for sample)	

Step 1: Cross-stitch (2 strands)

Anchor			DMC	
1	·	⁄		White
4146	−	⁄	754	Peach-lt.
159	X	⁄	3325	Baby Blue-lt.
	O	⁄	3811	Turquoise-vy. lt.
117	△	⁄	341	Blue Violet-lt.
401	●	⁄	413	Pewter Gray-dk.

Step 2: Backstitch (1 strand)

401	⌐	413	Pewter Gray-dk.

Step 3: Mill Hill Glass Beads

▲	00968	Red
⁄	02006	Ice-blue
∴	02008	Sea Breeze

Momma's Little Angel Pinafore

Materials
Finished design
1 yd. lt. blue cotton fabric
2 yds. of ¾"-wide white satin ribbon
2¼ yds. of ½"-wide mint-green satin ribbon
2¼ yds. of ¼"-wide lt. blue satin ribbon
Thread: white and lt. blue
Tracing paper

Directions
1. Using tracing paper, make pattern for bodice and pocket. Note: bodice pieces are cut on the fold. See page 131 for patterns.

2. Center bodice pattern over cross-stitch design and cut one. Center pocket pattern over cross-stitch design and cut one. Center pocket pattern over plain white Aida and cut one for lining.

(continued on page 118)

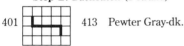

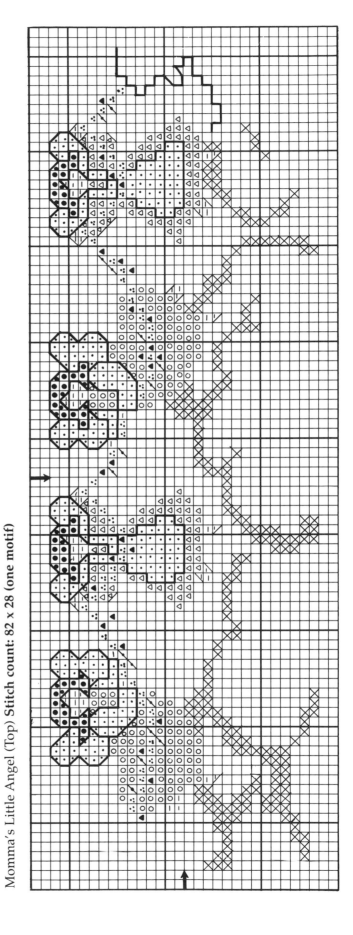

Momma's Little Angel (Top) Stitch count: 82 x 28 (one motif)

Floral Bath

Stitched on white Cashel linen 28 over 2 threads, the finished design size is 8¾" x 3¼". The fabric was cut 15" x 10".

Fabric	Design Size
Aida 11	11⅛" x 4⅛"
Aida 18	6⅞" x 2½"
Hardanger	5⅝" x 2"

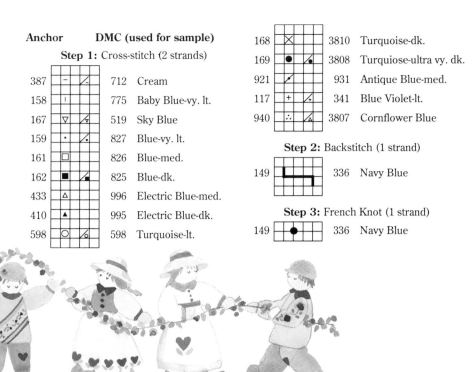

Anchor		DMC (used for sample)	
	Step 1: Cross-stitch (2 strands)		
387		712	Cream
158		775	Baby Blue-vy. lt.
167		519	Sky Blue
159		827	Blue-vy. lt.
161		826	Blue-med.
162		825	Blue-dk.
433		996	Electric Blue-med.
410		995	Electric Blue-dk.
598		598	Turquoise-lt.
168		3810	Turquoise-dk.
169		3808	Turquoise-ultra vy. dk.
921		931	Antique Blue-med.
117		341	Blue Violet-lt.
940		3807	Cornflower Blue
	Step 2: Backstitch (1 strand)		
149		336	Navy Blue
	Step 3: French Knot (1 strand)		
149		336	Navy Blue

Floral Bath (Left) Stitch count: 123 x 45

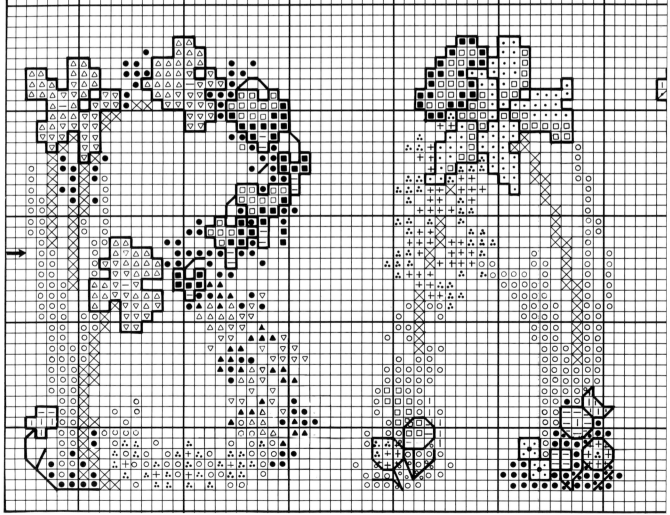

(continued from page 115)

3. From blue fabric, cut three bodice pieces and one skirt piece that is 20" long by the width of the fabric.

4. Cut each ribbon color into four 18" strips. Layer each group as follows: white, green and blue, pinning together and setting aside for straps.

5. Place pocket pieces right sides together and stitch around top and sides. Turn, press and stitch bottom closed. Lay a length of mint-green ribbon under design on pocket. Center a length of blue ribbon over green ribbon. Fold ribbon ends to back and pin in place. Make a

small bow from blue ribbon and tack in center. Set aside.

6. Using the skirt fabric, press bottom edge under ¼" and then again 2". Stitch hem. Sew up back seam. Run a gathering stitch along top edge of skirt. Mark top edge in quarters.

7. Place the design bodice and one fabric bodice right sides together. Sew along side seams. Repeat with remaining bodice pieces for lining.

8. Match end of ribbon straps to upper raw edges of bodice front, right sides together. Pin ¼" in from corner with straps hanging down over bodice front. Repeat for back straps.

9. Place right sides of bodice and lining together and stitch with a ¼" seam on all except lower edge. Clip curved edges. Turn and press.

10. Gather skirt to fit around bodice, matching quarter marks to center front and side seams. Sew right sides of skirt and outside bodice together with a ¼" seam. Remove gathering threads if they show.

11. Fold lower edge of bodice lining under ¼" and slip-stitch to inside of skirt, covering gathered edges.

12. Sew pocket onto front of pinafore.

Floral Bath (Right)

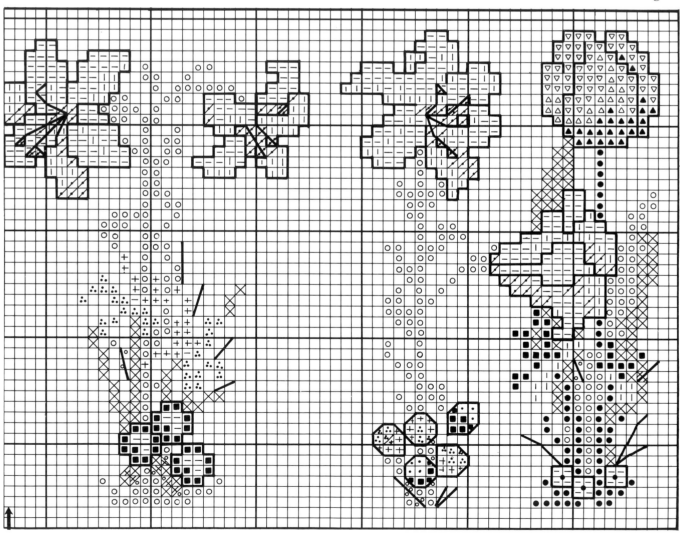

118

Lilacs

Stitched on white Cashel linen 28 over 2 threads, the finished design size is 3⅛" x 3½". The fabric was cut 8" x 16". See photo on page 119.

Fabric	Design Size
Aida 11	4" x 4½"
Aida 18	2½" x 2¾"
Hardanger	2" x 2¼"

Anchor		DMC (used for sample)	
Step 1: Cross-stitch (2 strands)			
118	I	340	Blue Violet-med.
119	O	333	Blue Violet-dk.
940	■	792	Cornflower Blue-dk.
167	−	598	Turquoise-lt.
168	△	597	Turquoise
169	✕	3809	Turquoise-vy. dk.

Teal-Fringed Potpourri Bag

Materials
Finished design
6½" x 9" piece of Cashel white linen; thread
⅜ yd. of teal taffeta; thread
1 yd. of lt. teal cording
¼ yd. of teal fringe
1 yd. of 2"-wide lt. teal sheer ribbon
1 package potpourri

Directions
1. Trim stitched piece to match linen back with design centered on lower

(continued on page 122)

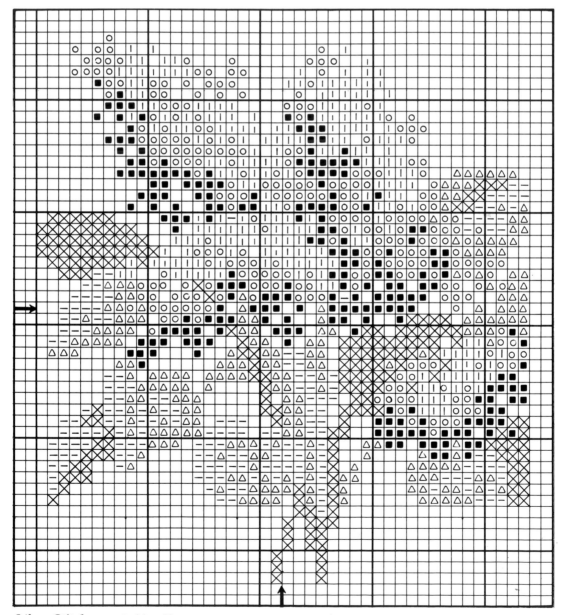

Lilacs **Stitch count: 44 x 49**

Blue Roses

Stitched on white Cashel linen 28 over 2 threads, the finished design size is 5¾" x 6¼". The fabric was cut 12" x 12". See photo on page 121.

Fabric	Design Size
Aida 11	7⅜" x 7⅞"
Aida 18	4½" x 4⅞"
Hardanger	3⅝" x 4"

Blue Roses Pillow

Materials
Finished design trimmed to 10" square
¾ yd. white glitter organza
½ yd. white broadcloth; matching thread
1½ yds. lt. teal 2"-wide sheer ribbon
Small bag of stuffing
Lt. blue fabric dye

Directions
1. Dye organza following manufacturer's instructions. Let dry.

2. From white fabric, cut three 10" squares. Place stitched piece and one white square wrong sides together and sew a seam around edges. Repeat with remaining white squares.

3. Cut organza into three 8" x 45" strips. Sew together at short ends, forming a circle. Fold in half lengthwise and press. Sew a gathering stitch along raw edge. Pull threads, gathering ruffle to fit around pillow. Pin in place around front of pillow with ruffle pointing to middle. Stitch in place, easing as you go.

4. Place pillow back on top of ruffles. *Note: use tape or pins to keep ruffles inside while attaching back.* Sew around edges, leaving a 4" opening. Clip corners and turn. Stuff firmly and whipstitch closed.

5. Leaving a 6" tail, gather sheer ribbon to make a rose and tack to bottom right corner of pillow. Continue around pillow with ribbon, tacking as you go.

(continued from page 120)

portion (about 1½" up from bottom).

2. Pin fringe to bottom of bag front with fringe pointing up. Place right side of plain linen back over design piece and stitch around sides and bottom, keeping the fringe inside. Turn. Press raw edge under ½".

3. From taffeta, cut 2 linings 6½" x 12". Place right sides together and sew around sides and bottom. Turn top of lining out about 2" and press. Slide lining into sachet bag. Lining will be taller than bag.

4. Pleat sheer ribbon to go around top of bag. Insert between lining and bag and hand-sew into place.

5. Fill bag with potpourri and tie with cording.

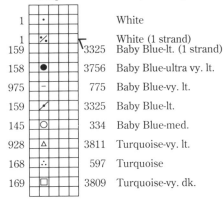

Anchor		DMC (used for sample)
Step 1: Cross-stitch (2 strands)		
1	·	White
1	⁄	White (1 strand)
159		3325 Baby Blue-lt. (1 strand)
158	●	3756 Baby Blue-ultra vy. lt.
975	−	775 Baby Blue-vy. lt.
159	╱	3325 Baby Blue-lt.
145	O	334 Baby Blue-med.
928	△	3811 Turquoise-vy. lt.
168	∴	597 Turquoise
169	□	3809 Turquoise-vy. dk.

Blue Roses (Left) **Stitch count: 81 x 87**

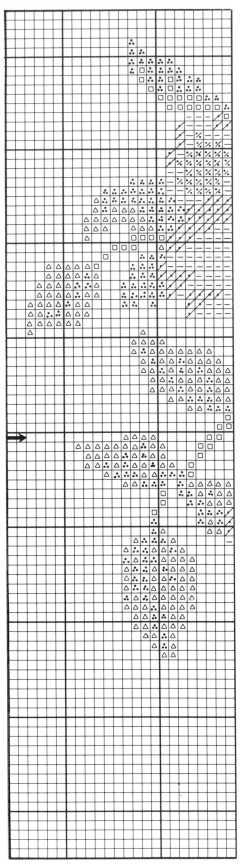

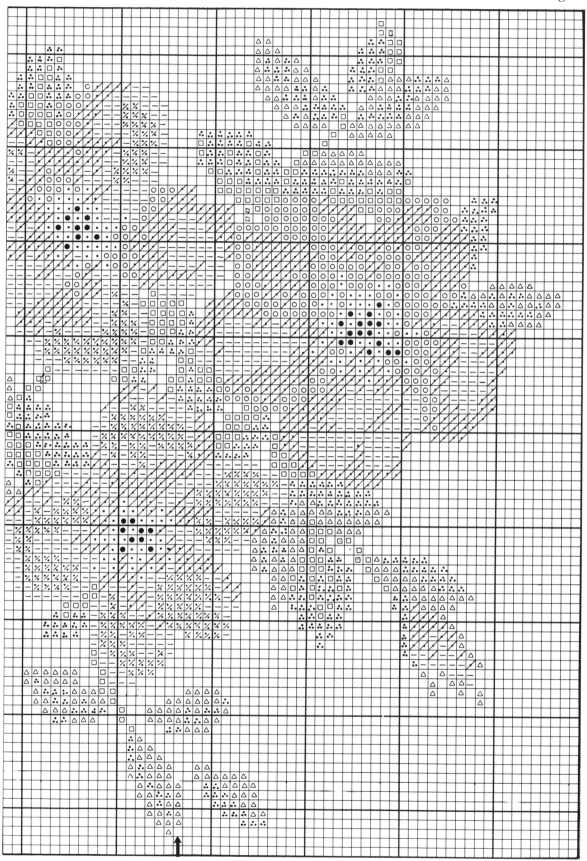

Spring Fling

Stitched on white Murano 30 over 2 threads, the finished design size is 4⅜" x 5⅞". The fabric was cut 10" x 12". See graph on page 126.

Fabric	Design Size
Aida 11	6" x 8⅛"
Aida 14	4¾" x 6⅜"
Aida 18	3⅝" x 5"
Hardanger	3" x 4"

Anchor		DMC (used for sample)	

Step 1: Cross-stitch (2 strands)

Anchor		DMC	
1	·		White
4146	l	754	Peach-lt.
868	◇	758	Terra Cotta-lt.
893	▽	224	Shell Pink-lt.
158	+	775	Baby Blue-vy. lt.
159	△	3325	Baby Blue-lt.
145	▲	334	Baby Blue-med.
147	⊠	312	Navy Blue-lt.
118	∷	340	Blue Violet-med.
119	●	333	Blue Violet-dk.
168	☐	597	Turquoise
169	■	3809	Turquoise-vy. dk.
942	U	738	Tan-vy. lt. (1 strand each)
		001HL	Silver Balger Blending Filament
397	−	762	Pearl Gray-vy. lt.
398	○	415	Pearl Gray
400	∴	414	Steel Gray-dk.
236	◆	3799	Pewter Gray-vy. dk.

Step 2: Backstitch (1 strand)

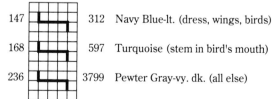

147	312	Navy Blue-lt. (dress, wings, birds)
168	597	Turquoise (stem in bird's mouth)
236	3799	Pewter Gray-vy. dk. (all else)

Spring Fling Lamp

Materials
Finished design
Lamp hardware kit
Wooden lamp base
Shade designing kit
½ yd. of fabric of choice
Decorative trim (enough for top and bottom of shade)
½ yd. of cording
Acrylic paint to match design and fabric
Satin-finish spray
Spray adhesive
Hot glue gun and glue sticks

Directions
1. Paint lamp base, leaving one side panel unfinished (this will be the front). Let dry. Spray twice with satin finish.

2. Cut 2 fabric panels to fit sides of lamp base, folding edges under to finish. Using spray adhesive, attach fabric to sides.

3. Trim design piece to fit front of lamp base and attach with spray adhesive. Trim cording to go across top and bottom edge of design and glue in place.

4. Following manufacturer's instructions, cover the lamp shade. Add trim along top and bottom of shade as desired.

5. Assemble lamp according to manufacturer's instructions.

Spring Fling **Stitch count: 66 x 89**

Bouquet Basket

Stitched on white Cashel linen 28 over 2 threads, the finished design size is 6½" x 7⅛". The fabric was cut 14" x 14". See photo on page 127.

Fabric	Design Size
Aida 11	8¼" x 9⅛"
Aida 18	5" x 5½"
Hardanger	4⅛" x 4½"

Anchor		DMC (used for sample)	

Step 1: Cross-stitch (2 strands)

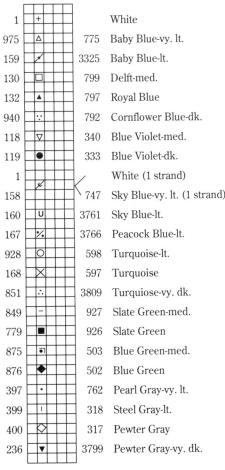

1	+		White
975	△	775	Baby Blue-vy. lt.
159	╱	3325	Baby Blue-lt.
130	▢	799	Delft-med.
132	▲	797	Royal Blue
940	∷	792	Cornflower Blue-dk.
118	▽	340	Blue Violet-med.
119	●	333	Blue Violet-dk.
1	╱		White (1 strand)
158		747	Sky Blue-vy. lt. (1 strand)
160	U	3761	Sky Blue-lt.
167	╱	3766	Peacock Blue-lt.
928	○	598	Turquoise-lt.
168	✕	597	Turquoise
851	∴	3809	Turquiose-vy. dk.
849	–	927	Slate Green-med.
779	■	926	Slate Green
875	⬓	503	Blue Green-med.
876	◆	502	Blue Green
397	·	762	Pearl Gray-vy. lt.
399	I	318	Steel Gray-lt.
400	◇	317	Pewter Gray
236	▼	3799	Pewter Gray-vy. dk.

Step 2: Backstitch (1 strand)

| 236 | | 3799 | Pewter Gray-vy. dk. |

Bouquet Basket Pillow

Materials
Finished design centered and trimmed to 12" x 13"
12" x 13" piece of white linen; matching thread
1 yd. of white glitter organza
3 yds. of 1½-wide lt. blue wired ribbon; matching thread
Stuffing

Directions
1. Cut organza into four 9" x 45" strips. Fold each strip in half lengthwise. Bring each corner down to the fold. Cut off corners and unfold.

2. Place two strips right sides together and sew one corner. Fold top strip back and sew third strip to other corner. Fold third strip back and sew last strip to corner. Bring ends together and sew last corner. *Note: you should now have a continuous ruffle.* Clip corners and turn right side out. Press.

3. Sew a gathering stitch along inside edge of ruffle. Set aside.

4. Using 1½ yds. of ribbon, pull wire out of both edges. Place around top inside edge of design piece, lining up edges and mitering corners. Topstitch both edges down.

5. Pull gathering thread around ruffle and adjust to fit around pillow top. Pin ruffle around pillow top, right sides together, with ruffle laying on top of design. Place linen piece face down on top of ruffles and sew around edges, leaving a 4" opening. Clip corners, turn and stuff firmly. Whipstitch opening closed.

6. With remaining ribbon, tie a bow with long tails. Attach bow to top left corner and cascade tails along top and side, tacking about every 3".

Bouquet Basket (Left)
Stitch count: 91 x 100

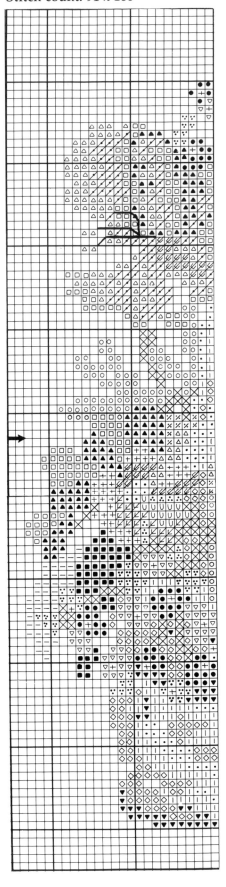

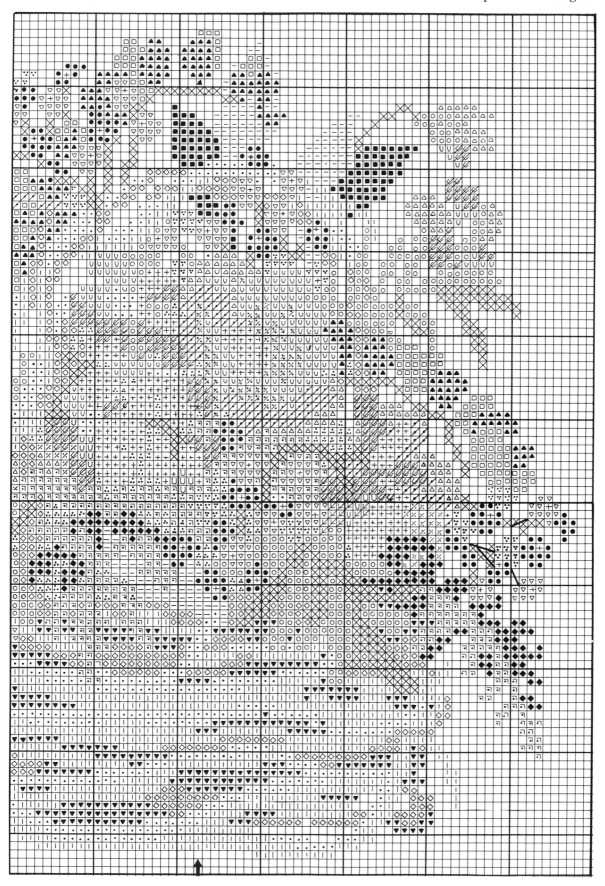

Welcome to Our Home

Stitched on white Belfast linen 32 over 2 threads, the finished design size is 15⅛" x 9¼". The fabric was cut 22" x 16". Graph begins on page 132.

Fabric	Design Size
Aida 11	22" x 13½"
Aida 14	17¼" x 10⅝"
Aida 18	13½" x 8¼"
Hardanger	11" x 6¾"

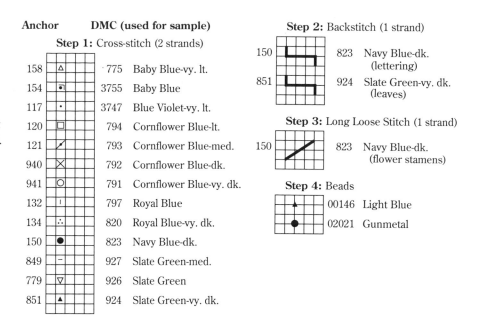

Anchor		DMC (used for sample)	
Step 1: Cross-stitch (2 strands)			
158	△	775	Baby Blue-vy. lt.
154	▣	3755	Baby Blue
117	·	3747	Blue Violet-vy. lt.
120	□	794	Cornflower Blue-lt.
121	╱	793	Cornflower Blue-med.
940	✕	792	Cornflower Blue-dk.
941	○	791	Cornflower Blue-vy. dk.
132	Ɩ	797	Royal Blue
134	∴	820	Royal Blue-vy. dk.
150	●	823	Navy Blue-dk.
849	–	927	Slate Green-med.
779	▽	926	Slate Green
851	▲	924	Slate Green-vy. dk.

Step 2: Backstitch (1 strand)

150	823	Navy Blue-dk. (lettering)
851	924	Slate Green-vy. dk. (leaves)

Step 3: Long Loose Stitch (1 strand)

150	823	Navy Blue-dk. (flower stamens)

Step 4: Beads

▲	00146	Light Blue
●	02021	Gunmetal

Momma's Little Angel Pinafore Pattern
(from page 115)

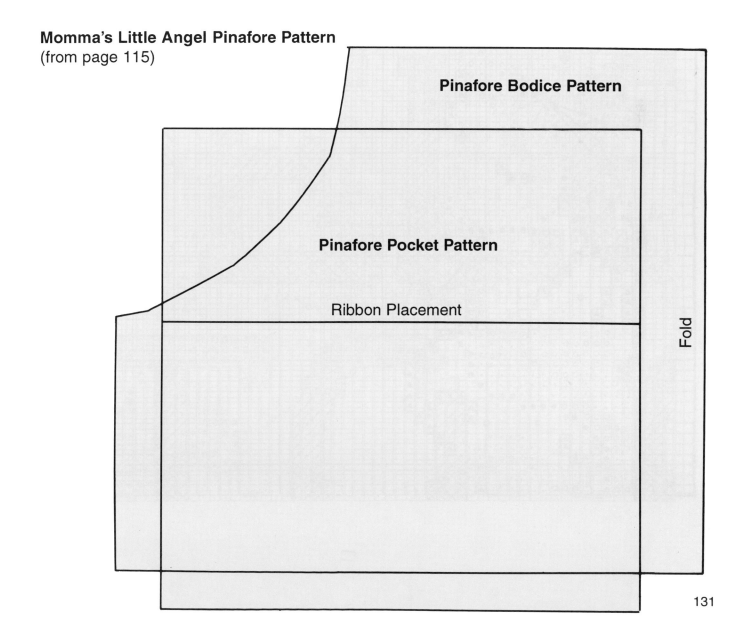

Pinafore Bodice Pattern

Pinafore Pocket Pattern

Ribbon Placement

Fold

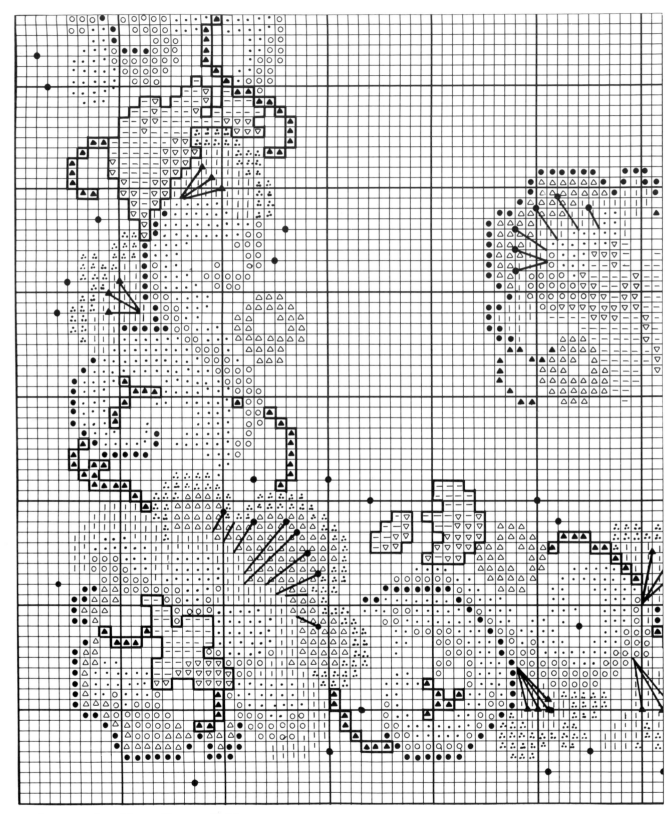

Welcome to Our Home (Bottom Left)

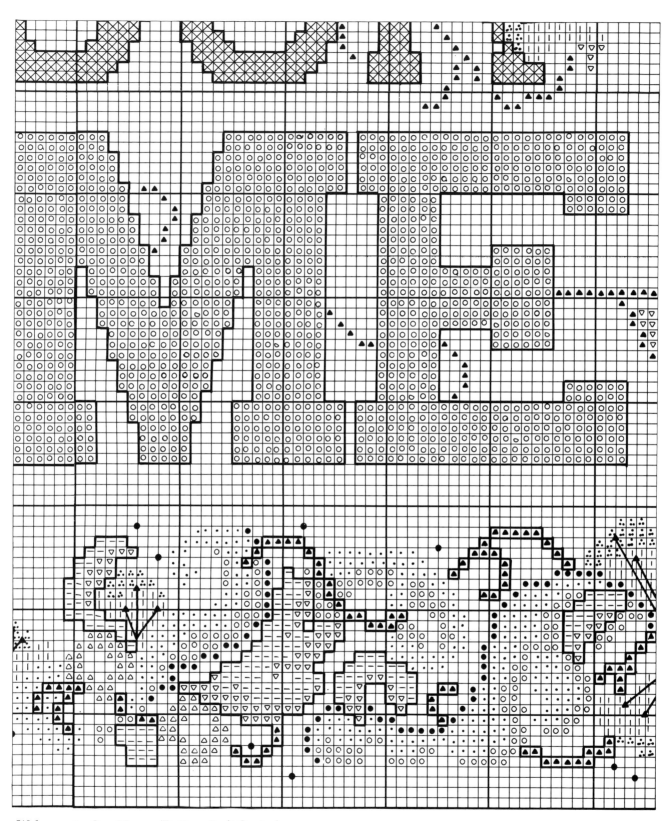

Welcome to Our Home (Bottom Left Center)

Welcome to Our Home (Bottom Right Center)

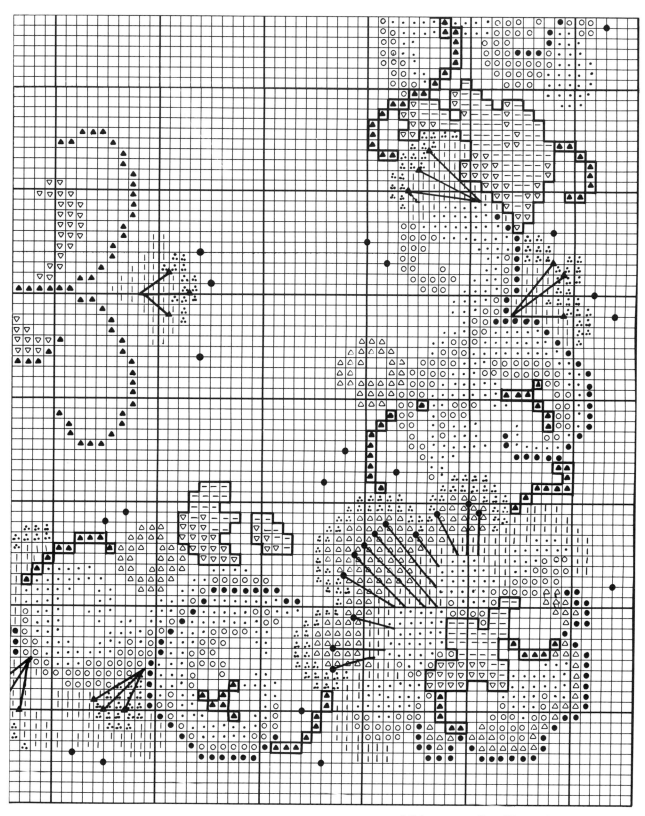

Welcome to Our Home (Bottom Right)

General Instructions

Fabric for Cross-stitch
Counted cross-stitch is usually worked on even-weave fabrics. These fabrics are manufactured specifically for counted-thread embroidery and are woven with the same number of vertical as horizontal threads per inch. Because the number of threads in the fabric is equal in each direction, each stitch will be the same size. The number of threads per inch in even-weave fabrics determines the size of a finished design. Fabrics used for models are identified in sample information by color, name, and thread count per inch.

Preparing Fabric
Cut fabric at least 3" larger on all sides than finished design size or cut as indicated in sample information to ensure enough space for project assembly. A 3" margin is the minimum amount of space that allows for comfortably finishing the edges of the design. To prevent fraying, whipstitch or machine-zigzag along raw edges or apply liquid fray preventer.

Needles for Cross-stitch
Needles should slip easily through fabric holes without piercing fabric threads. For fabric with 11 or fewer threads per inch, use a tapestry needle size 24; for 14 threads per inch, use a tapestry needle size 24 or 26; for 18 or more threads per inch, use a tapestry needle size 26. Never leave needle in design area of fabric. It may leave rust or permanent impression on fabric.

Floss
All numbers and color names are cross-referenced between Anchor and DMC brands of floss. Use 18" lengths of floss. For best coverage, separate strands. Dampen with wet sponge. Then put together number of strands called for in color code.

Centering the Design
Fold the fabric in half horizontally, then vertically. Place a pin in the fold point to mark the center. Locate the center of the design on the graph by following the vertical and horizontal arrows in the left and bottom margins. Begin stitching all designs at the center point of graph and fabric, unless the instructions indicate otherwise.

Securing the Floss
Insert needle up from the underside of the fabric at starting point. Hold 1" of thread behind the fabric and stitch over it, securing with the first few stitches. To finish thread, run under four or more stitches on the back of the design. Never knot floss, unless working on clothing. Another method of securing floss is the waste knot. Knot floss and insert needle from the right side of the fabric about 1" from design area. Work several stitches over the thread to secure. Cut off the knot later.

Stitching Method
For smooth stitches, use the push-and-pull method. Starting on wrong side of fabric, push needle straight up, pulling floss completely through to right side. Reinsert needle and bring it back straight down, pulling needle and floss completely through to back of fabric. Keep floss flat but do not pull thread tight. For even stitches, tension should be consistent throughout.

Carrying Floss
To carry floss, weave floss under the previously worked stitches on the back. Do not carry thread across any fabric that is not or will not be stitched. Loose threads, especially dark ones, will show through the fabric.

Cleaning Completed Work
When stitching is complete, soak it in cold water with a mild soap for five to 10 minutes. Rinse well and roll in a towel to remove excess water. Do not wring. Place work face down on a dry towel and iron on warm setting until dry.

Cross-stitch
Stitches are done in a row or, if necessary, one at a time in an area. Stitching is done by coming up through a hole between woven threads at A. Then, go down at B, the hole diagonally across from A. Come back up at C and down at D, etc. Complete the top stitches to create an "X". All top stitches should lie in the same direction. Come up at E and go down at B, come up at C and go down at F, etc.

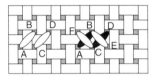

Backstitch
Pull the needle through at the point marked "A". Then go down one opening to the right, at the point marked "B". Then, come back up at the point marked "C". Now, go down one opening to the right, this time at "A".

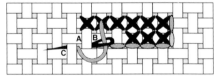

French Knot
Bring needle up at A, using two strands of embroidery floss. Loosely wrap floss once around needle. Place needle at B, next to A. Pull floss taut as you push needle down through fabric. Carry floss across back of work between knots.

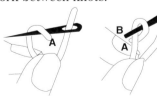

Silk Ribbon

To complete each project, you will need to purchase silk ribbon. The colors are outlined in the corresponding stitch guide. The majority of the work is done in 4mm ribbon. Where 7mm is used, there is a 7 before the ribbon color number. Before you begin, you should press the silk ribbon using low heat to remove any creases. Cut the ribbon into 18" lengths to reduce the chance of the silk ribbon fraying while stitching. Because of the delicate nature of silk ribbon, it can easily become worn, losing some of its body. If this happens, moisten the silk ribbon and it will self-restore. Because silk is a natural fiber, there may be slight color hue differences between strands.

Fabric for Ribbon

All designs can be stitched on specified fabric or fabric of your choice. It is recommended that you stretch your fabric taut on a hoop before you begin stitching.

Needles for Ribbon

The barrel of the needle must create a hole large enough for the silk ribbon to pass through. The ribbon will hide the hole made by the needle. If the silk ribbon does not pull through the fabric easily enough, a larger needle is needed. Also, the eye of the needle must be large enough for the silk ribbon to lay flat when threaded. Use a needle pack that includes chenille needles in sizes 18 to 22. Use a regular embroidery needle when stitching with DMC floss.

Method of Silk Ribbon Embroidery

Threading and Locking Silk Ribbon

Pull about 3" of silk ribbon through the eye of the needle. Pierce the 3" portion of silk ribbon about ½" from the end. Pull back on the opposite end until it locks securely around the eye of the needle; see Diagram 1.

Diagram 1

Knotting the End of the Silk Ribbon

To create a soft knot prior to stitching, drape the silk ribbon in a circular manner to position the end of the silk ribbon perpendicular to the tip of the needle. Pierce the end of the silk ribbon with the needle, sliding the needle through the silk ribbon as if to make a short basting stitch. Pull the needle and silk ribbon through the stitched portion to form a knot at the ribbon end; see Diagram 2.

Diagram 2

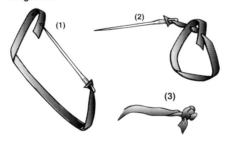

Manipulating the Silk Ribbon

One of the most important aspects of silk ribbon embroidery is manipulation of the silk ribbon. For most stitches, the silk ribbon must be kept flat, smooth and loose. You must use your thumb and the needle to manipulate the ribbon as you stitch or the silk ribbon may curl and fold, affecting the appearance of your picture; see Diagram 3. Follow the numerical order of stitches according to the stitching guide for each project. Untwist the silk ribbon during each stitch and use the needle to lift and straighten the ribbon. Pull the silk ribbon gently to allow the stitches to lie softly on top of the fabric. Exact stitch placement is not critical, but you will want to make sure any placement marks are covered by silk ribbon stitches. You may add a few extra petals or leaves by using any leftover ribbon. There are no mistakes, only variations. Be creative with your stitching!

Diagram 3

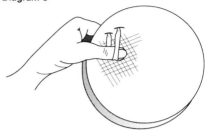

To End Stitching

Secure your stitches in place for each flower or small area before beginning a new area. *Do not* drag the ribbon from one area to another. Tie a slip knot on the wrong side of your needlework to secure the stitch in place and end ribbon.

Transferring Patterns Using Dressmaker's Carbon

Purchase a package of dressmaker's carbon at your local notions store. Using provided project transfer diagrams, follow manufacturer's instructions to transfer design from book pages to fabric. For transferring on black fabric, transfer design first on a white piece of paper and then trace with a dressmaker's pen.

Caring for Your Projects

It is recommended to spot-clean only, but due to the need to continually clean clothing, hand-wash with mild dishwashing detergent. If needed, carefully press around embroidered design.

Stitches

Beading Stitch

Using one strand of floss, come up through fabric. Slide the bead(s) on the needle and push the needle back down through fabric. Knot off each bead.

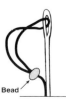

Couched Ribbon Stitch

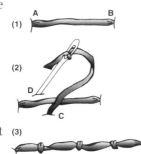

1. Complete a straight stitch base by coming up at A and going down at B. Make sure the ribbon is flat and loose.
2. Make a short tight straight stitch across the ribbon base to "couch" the straight stitch. Come up at C on one side of the ribbon. Go down at D on the opposite side of the ribbon. The tight short stitch across the ribbon will cause the ribbon to gather and pucker. Couch at varying intervals.
3. Completed Couched Ribbon Stitch.

Cretan Stitch

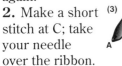

1. Come up at A; go down at B, making a short straight stitch and come up again.
2. Make a short stitch at C; take your needle over the ribbon.
3. Come up again at D. Continue Steps 2 and 3 until area is complete. Take needle to back of fabric to finish.

Curved Whipstitch

1. Come up at A and down at B.
2. Come back up at A; wrap the ribbon around the straight stitch, bringing it over the top of the stitch and sliding the needle under the straight stitch. Repeat two times.

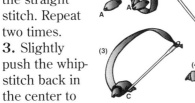

3. Slightly push the whip-stitch back in the center to allow you to go down at C, under the whipstitch. This will cause the whip-stitch to curve.
4. Completed Curved Whipstitch.

French Knot—Ribbon

1. Bring needle up through fabric; smoothly wrap ribbon once around needle.
2. Hold ribbon securely off to one side and push needle down through fabric close to the starting point.
3. Completed French Knots.

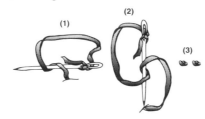

Fly Stitch

1. Bring the needle up at A. Keep the ribbon flat, untwisted and full. Put the needle down through the fabric at B and up at C, keeping the ribbon under the needle forming a "U".
2. Pull the ribbon through, leaving the ribbon to drape loose and full. To hold the ribbon in place, go down on other side of ribbon at D, forming a straight stitch over loop. The length of the straight stitch may vary according to the desired effect.
3. Completed Fly Stitch.

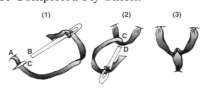

Japanese Ribbon Stitch

1. Come up through fabric at the starting point of stitch. Lay the ribbon flat on the fabric. At the end of the stitch, pierce the ribbon with the needle. Slowly pull the length of the ribbon through to the back, allowing the ends of the ribbon to curl. If the ribbon is pulled too tight, the effect of the stitch will be lost. Vary the petals and leaves by adjusting the length, the tension of the ribbon before piercing, the position of piercing, and how loosely or tightly the ribbon is pulled down through itself.
2. Completed Japanese Ribbon Stitch.

Feather Stitch

1. Come up at A. Go down at B and back up at C, keeping the floss/ribbon under the needle to hold it in a "V" shape. Pull flat.
2. For second stitch, go down at D and back up at E.
3. Completed Feather Stitch.

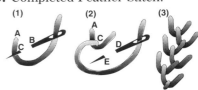

Lazy Daisy

1. Bring the needle up at A. Keep the ribbon flat, untwisted and full. Put the needle down through fabric at B and up through at C, keeping the ribbon under the needle to form a loop. Pull the ribbon through, leaving the loop loose and full. To hold the loop in place, go down on other side of ribbon near C, forming a straight stitch over loop.

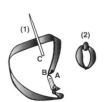

2. Completed Lazy Daisy.

Spider Web Rose

1. Using two strands of matching color or white floss or sewing thread, securely work straight stitches to form five spokes. These are your anchor stitches to create the rose with ribbon.
2. Bring the piece of ribbon up through the center of the spokes.
3. & 4. Weave the ribbon over one spoke and under the next spoke, continuing around in one direction (clockwise or counter-clockwise), until the spokes are covered. When weaving, keep the ribbon loose and allow it to twist. To end, stitch down through fabric along the last row of petals.

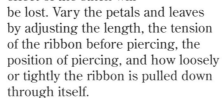

5. Completed Spider Web Rose.

Stem Stitch

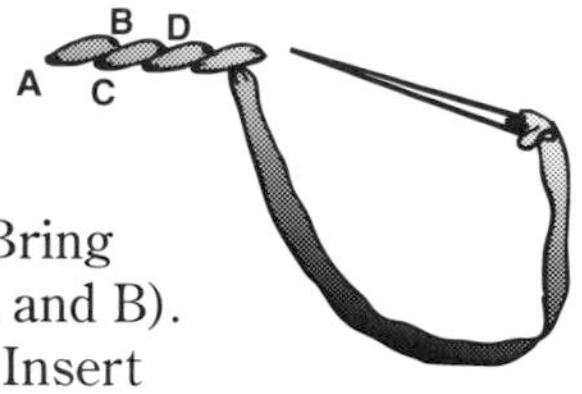

Working from left to right, make slightly slanting stitches along the line of the stem. Come up at A and insert needle through fabric at B. Bring needle up at C (halfway between A and B). Make all stitches the same length. Insert needle through fabric at D (half the length of the stitch beyond B). Bring needle up at the middle of previous stitch and continue in the same manner.

Straight Stitch

This stitch may be taut or loose, depending on desired effect.
1. Come up at A. Go down at B, keeping the ribbon flat.
2. Completed Straight Stitch.

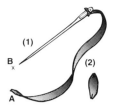

Metric Equivalency Chart

MM-Millimetres   CM-Centimetres

INCHES TO MILLIMETRES AND CENTIMETRES

INCHES	MM	CM	INCHES	CM	INCHES	CM
⅛	3	0.3	9	22.9	30	76.2
¼	6	0.6	10	25.4	31	78.7
½	13	1.3	12	30.5	33	83.8
⅝	16	1.6	13	33.0	34	86.4
¾	19	1.9	14	35.6	35	88.9
⅞	22	2.2	15	38.1	36	91.4
1	25	2.5	16	40.6	37	94.0
1¼	32	3.2	17	43.2	38	96.5
1½	38	3.8	18	45.7	39	99.1
1¾	44	4.4	19	48.3	40	101.6
2	51	5.1	20	50.8	41	104.1
2½	64	6.4	21	53.3	42	106.7
3	76	7.6	22	55.9	43	109.2
3½	89	8.9	23	58.4	44	111.8
4	102	10.2	24	61.0	45	114.3
4½	114	11.4	25	63.5	46	116.8
5	127	12.7	26	66.0	47	119.4
6	152	15.2	27	68.6	48	121.9
7	178	17.8	28	71.1	49	124.5
8	203	20.3	29	73.7	50	127.0

YARDS TO METRES

YARDS	METRES	YARDS	METRES	YARDS	METRES	YARDS	METRES	YARDS	METRES
⅛	0.11	2⅛	1.94	4⅛	3.77	6⅛	5.60	8⅛	7.43
¼	0.23	2¼	2.06	4¼	3.89	6¼	5.72	8¼	7.54
⅜	0.34	2⅜	2.17	4⅜	4.00	6⅜	5.83	8⅜	7.66
½	0.46	2½	2.29	4½	4.11	6½	5.94	8½	7.77
⅝	0.57	2⅝	2.40	4⅝	4.23	6⅝	6.06	8⅝	7.89
¾	0.69	2¾	2.51	4¾	4.34	6¾	6.17	8¾	8.00
⅞	0.80	2⅞	2.63	4⅞	4.46	6⅞	6.29	8⅞	8.12
1	0.91	3	2.74	5	4.57	7	6.40	9	8.23
1⅛	1.03	3⅛	2.86	5⅛	4.69	7⅛	6.52	9⅛	8.34
1¼	1.14	3¼	2.97	5¼	4.80	7¼	6.63	9¼	8.46
1⅜	1.26	3⅜	3.09	5⅜	4.91	7⅜	6.74	9⅜	8.57
1½	1.37	3½	3.20	5½	5.03	7½	6.86	9½	8.69
1⅝	1.49	3⅝	3.31	5⅝	5.14	7⅝	6.97	9⅝	8.80
1¾	1.60	3¾	3.43	5¾	5.26	7¾	7.09	9¾	8.92
1⅞	1.71	3⅞	3.54	5⅞	5.37	7⅞	7.20	9⅞	9.03
2	1.83	4	3.66	6	5.49	8	7.32	10	9.14

Index